PERGAMON INSTITUTE OF ENGLISH (OXFORD)

Council of Europe Modern Languages Project

ACROSS THE THRESHOLD

Readings from the Modern Languages
Projects of the Council of Europe

Other Titles in the Series

The Council of Europe was established by ten nations on 5 May 1949, since when its membership has progressively increased to twenty-one. Its aim is "to achieve a greater unity between its Members for the purpose of safeguarding and realising the ideals and principles which are their common heritage and facilitating their economic and social progress". This aim is pursued by discussion of questions of common concern and by agreements and common action in economic, social, cultural, scientific, legal and administrative matters.

The Council for Cultural Co-operation was set up by the Committee of Ministers of the Council of Europe on 1 January 1962 to draw up proposals for the cultural policy of the Council of Europe, to co-ordinate and give effect to the overall cultural programme of the organization and to allocate the resources of the Cultural Fund. All the member governments of the Council of Europe, together with the Holy See and Finland which have acceded to the European Cultural Convention, are represented on the Council for Cultural Co-operation.

The aim of the work carried out by the Council for Cultural Co-operation in the area of modern language learning is to encourage the development of *understanding, co-operation* and *mobility* among Europeans by improving and broadening the learning of *modern languages* by all sections of the population. This aim will be pursued.

- by making generally available the basic tools for the systematic planning, construction and conduct of learning programmes geared to the needs and motivations of the learners and to the changing requirements of society;
- by helping to prepare teachers to play their proper roles in such programmes,
- and by further developing a framework for close and effective international co-operation in the promotion of language learning.

For this purpose, and under the authority of the Council for Cultural Co-operation, a number of studies have been prepared, some of which are being published in this Council of European Modern Language Series. However, the opinions expressed in the studies written in this framework are not to be regarded as reflecting the policy of any government, of the Committee of Ministers or the Secretary General of the Council of Europe.

Applications for reproduction and translation should be addressed to the Director of Education, Culture and Sport, Council of Europe, Strasbourg (France).

ACROSS THE THRESHOLD

Readings from the Modern Languages
Projects of the Council of Europe

by

J A van Ek

University of Groningen, Holland

and

J L M Trim

Centre for Information on Language Teaching & Research, London

Published for and on behalf of the

COUNCIL OF EUROPE

by

PERGAMON PRESS

OXFORD · NEW YORK · TORONTO · SYDNEY · PARIS · FRANKFURT

U.K.	Pergamon Press Ltd., Headington Hill Hall, Oxford OX3 0BW, England
U.S.A.	Pergamon Press Inc., Maxwell House, Fairview Park, Elmsford, New York 10523, U.S.A.
CANADA	Pergamon Press Canada Ltd., Suite 104, 150 Consumers Road, Willowdale, Ontario M2J 1P9, Canada
AUSTRALIA	Pergamon Press (Aust.) Pty. Ltd., P.O. Box 544, Potts Point, N.S.W. 2011, Australia
FRANCE	Pergamon Press SARL, 24 rue des Ecoles, 75240 Paris, Cedex 05, France
FEDERAL REPUBLIC OF GERMANY	Pergamon Press GmbH, Hammerweg 6, D-6242 Kronberg-Taunus, Federal Republic of Germany

First edition 1984

Library of Congress Cataloguing in Publication Data

Main entry under title:
Across the threshold.
(Council of Europe modern languages project)
Bibliography: p.
1. Languages, Modern — Study and teaching — Europe — Addresses, essays, lectures. I. Ek, Jan Ate van. II. Trim, J. L. M. (John Leslie Melville) III. Council of Europe. IV. Series.
PB38.E8A3   1984   418′.007′104   83–25747

British Library Cataloguing in Publication Data

Across the threshold.
1. Languages, Modern — Study and teaching
I. Ek, J. A. van   II. Trim, J. L. M.
418′.007   PB35

ISBN 0–08–029446–4

Printed and bound in Great Britain by
William Clowes Limited, Beccles and London

ACKNOWLEDGEMENTS

This reader brings together some of the key contributions to the Council of Europe Project No. 4, 'Modern Languages'. Behind them, however, stand many more. A brief look at the table of contents of the report on the CDCC Modern Languages Programme 1971–81 will suffice to show that the success of the project is the result of contributions from a great number of people. Their addresses, and, where appropriate, their institutions, figure in Appendix B to that report.

We should like to express our gratitude to these colleagues for their co-operation which has been indispensable to the success of the Project. This list is however by no means exhaustive and we are very much aware of our debt to the much larger number of colleagues who have helped us, but whom it is impossible to thank individually. All of them, by continuously and painstakingly building working relations among those concerned with language learning in Europe, have exemplified in the most meaningful and democratic way possible the full sense of the political objective that guides the programme: which is, to facilitate communication and interaction among Europeans of different mother tongues in the service of European mobility, mutual understanding and co-operation, and in order to overcome prejudice and discrimination.

CONTENTS

COUNCIL
OF EUROPE

CONSEIL
DE L' EUROPE

GENERAL INTRODUCTION

INTRODUCTION

The aim of this reader is to present in a compact form the approach to modern language learning and teaching developed in successive projects of the Council of Europe since 1971. This approach, which forms part of a more general movement to promote a more practical approach with effective communication as its goal, has been developed in a series of reports and papers, many of which are not easily accessible. Even in the series of seminal papers reprinted and published by Pergamon Press, the essentials of the approach are spread over several volumes, so that it is necessary for the reader to bring elements together from a number of different sources.

Our intention is, by selecting and editing key contributions in which important elements are clearly formulated, to present in a single volume of moderate compass the essentials of the approach for the benefit, particularly, of the practising teacher, but also of the many different contributors to the 'partnership for learning' on whose mutual understanding and co-operation the successful operation of our education systems depends: administrators, course designers and writers, examiners and inspectors, to name but a few.

The Council of Europe is an intergovernmental organization with its seat at Strasbourg in France, established soon after the Second World War to encourage co-operation among its member countries and to develop a European spirit which would make further fratricidal conflicts unthinkable. It has become a platform for member governments and institutions within member countries to demonstrate that their interests are better served through international co-operation than through unbridled competition or national self-sufficiency. The Council's work reported in this reader can only be understood in the light of the aims and objectives of the Council and the constraints and opportunities inherent in its status and organization.

The Council operates in the educational and cultural spheres under the terms of the European Cultural Convention the governments represented on the Council for Cultural Co-operation (CDCC) are: Austria, Belgium, Cyprus, Denmark, Finland, France, Federal Republic of Germany, Greece, Holy See, Iceland, Ireland, Italy, Liechtenstein, Luxembourg, Malta, Netherlands, Norway, Portugal, Spain, Sweden, Switzerland, Turkey, United Kingdom. The CDCC has always maintained a close concern for the promotion of modern language learning as a means to the freer movement of peoples and ideas in Europe. From 1962 to 1972 it mounted a major project to familiarize teachers with the findings of applied linguistics and the techniques of audio-visual teaching methods. The International Association for Applied Linguistics was established and fostered through its early years until, following the Second Congress in Cambridge, 1969, it became worldwide in coverage. Habits of international co-operation were formed and many valuable symposia held on all levels and aspects of language teaching. The work reported here was built upon the foundations laid in those years.

In 1971, the language programme of the Council took what turned out to be a decisive new direction, when a Group of Experts was asked to investigate the feasibility of a unit-credit scheme in modern languages for adult learners. The majority of the papers presented in this reader were written within that framework. A principal aim of the Council's work in the field of education, culture and sport is to promote the development of individuals who combine self-awareness and self-reliance with social awareness and social responsibility. Societies composed of individuals with these qualities are more likely to interact on the basis of mutual understanding and acceptance, and to maintain and develop strong, stable and yet dynamic democratic structures and processes. The reader of these pages will need to bear this concept constantly in mind when considering the arguments put forward.

The unit-credit concept was itself developed as a way of breaking down large global subjects, areas of knowledge or 'disciplines' which all learners are expected to study following a set path in the same way, into far smaller, relatively independent units which can be combined and sequenced in different ways according to the needs, motivations, characteristics and resources of different learners. 'Learner-centredness' means a profound change of emphasis and attitude for the teacher, who becomes, as it were, a minister rather than a priest, serving the learner by acting as a channel for access to knowledge and using professional skill to facilitate learning so long as it is necessary to do so, while fostering the learner's growth in awareness, proficiency and confidence towards the day when self-reliance can take over from teacher-reliance. The hieratic teacher, on the other hand, serves the 'language' with its literature as self-subsistent entities and initiates the learner into the necessary disciplines and mysteries. Since a skilled hieratic teacher will also take account of the learners' characteristics, exploit their motivations and be constrained by the available resources, as well as aiming ultimately to lead them (or one or two of them) to independent mastery, the difference between the two approaches may seem more apparent than real. However, the great difference lies in the approach to needs. In the first case the needs of the learner, carefully established in response to the circumstances of his present and future life, are paramount. In the second, they are irrelevant except in so far as they affect motivation. Accordingly, learner-centred education almost inevitably leads to the involvement of learners in decision-making, whilst subject-centred teaching tends to remain paternalistic and authoritarian. Not surprisingly, the first attitude is more common in adult education and the second in school. It is not by fortuitous coincidence that the approach identified with the Council of Europe Modern Languages Project was first developed in the field of adult education.

While unit-credit schemes as such are quite widely employed in adult, further and higher education, language units are still generally global in character: 'elementary French', 'advanced Chinese' etc., implying progress across the board. Languages for special purposes (LSP) e.g. 'English for banking', 'German for chemical engineers', are also frequently encountered. English usage avoids the assumption apparent in the French 'langues de specialité'. There are not generally restricted specialized languages (except where these may be established by explicit convention). The rules of syntax and morphology are not different from one special field to another, except as trivial consequences of essentially non-linguistic principles (e.g. the 'objectivity' of the agentless passive in scientific usage'). LSP is thus usually characterized above all by a specialized terminology. It would have been possible to devise a unit-credit scheme in terms simply of structural grading and defined vocabularies in the tradition established by 'le français fondamental'. In 1971 that would have been a relatively straightforward task, but uninteresting and probably sterile. The group preferred to break with direct grammatical and lexical specification and to seek a new basis for the definition of objectives. In doing so we were perhaps encouraged by Chomsky's demonstration that language acquisition and use could not be understood in terms of the insertion of lexical items into a set of structural frames. Some, at any rate, of us were rather more influenced by Hymes' teaching that there was much more than 'linguistic' (i.e. grammatical) competence to a 'communicative' competence, and by the older British traditions of J R Firth and H E Palmer.

The Council of Europe symposium on 'Linguistic content, means of evaluation and their interaction in the teaching and learning of modern languages in adult education', held at Rüschlikon, Switzerland on 3–7 May 1971, examined the problem from a situational standpoint. The language user employs his or her language in order to co-operate effectively with others in the manipulation of the situation in which (s)he is involved. If we can analyse the situations in which a particular learner can expect to be involved and the roles (s)he will be expected to play in them, we can, to a greater or lesser extent, predict what (s)he may be called upon to say, or to understand, or to read or write, and prepare him or her to do so.

Highly predictable situations are often characterized by the use of fixed formulaic expressions, as a glance at a phrase-book will show. Critics of a situational approach often criticize the results as 'mere phrasebook learning'. We can easily forget how much of our lives is passed in routine exchanges. But even they are rarely altogether stereotyped. 'Situational' dialogues, in their attempt to avoid boredom, often include individual, even idiosyncratic or facetious elements, so that the situational structure is lost sight of: the learner cannot see the wood for the trees. A situation is really a class of events, each perhaps unique but showing common properties. Many of these are in turn shared with other situations. We found it useful to supplement the situational analysis with a more general classification of the functions which language is called upon to perform and the notions it serves to express. Taken together, these products made it possible for teachers, learners, examiners, syllabus and course designers to consider in greater detail than before what they wanted to do with language, the activities involved and the knowledge and skills needed to act efficiently. The result has been on the one hand a greater consensus among members of the language teaching profession on a European – and indeed a global – scale on ways of arriving at statements of language learning objectives and on the other more conscious and explicit decision-making closer to the point of learning. An apparatus now exists with reference to which negotiation can take place.

The definition of objectives was given priority in the work of the project. Given well-defined objectives, we can see whether particular methods do or do not lead to this achievement. We can also evaluate methods of assessment, particularly with regard to their validity. Thus the essence of the 'Council of Europe approach' is a certain way of planning language learning, involving:

a.   establishing, and monitoring the development of, the needs, motivations, characteristics and resources of learners;
b.   setting up, and keeping under review, optimally worthwhile and feasible learning objectives, especially in terms of the knowledge and skills required in the predicted conditions and situations of language use;
c.   selecting and developing appropriate methods and materials which will bring the learners concerned to the operational proficiency aimed at;
d.   developing means of evaluation, both of the learners' achievement and of the effectiveness of the language teaching system, in order to provide appropriate feedback to the various members of the 'partnership for learning' which will enable them to improve future performance.

The main part of this reader is therefore arranged according to the concept of planning. In Chapter One, Trim sets out the case for teaching by units and explores some general characteristics of unit-credit schemes. In Chapter Two, Richterich explains the concept of 'needs' and its place in language learning systems development. Proposals by Chancerel and Richterich for an apparatus for consideration when identifying the needs of adult learners are then presented. Finally, van Ek presents the special considerations which apply to the identification of needs as applied to pupils in schools.

Chapter Three is devoted to the specification of objectives. Van Ek sets out the various dimensions of classification in terms of which operational language-learning objectives have been classified and then illustrates their application with sample extracts from *Threshold Level English* and *Waystage English*. Trim then gives a brief summary of progress made since 1975 towards a more comprehensive framework for the definition of language-learning objectives, taking into account the development of the learner as communicator and as learner, and also as an individual personality and a member of a social group.

In Chapter Four, Coste surveys the development of teaching method within the project. As he points out, the Expert Group approached this aspect with great caution, believing decisions on the method and materials to be used by learners to depend on their objectives, learner type and available resources. It would seem quite alien to the spirit of the enterprise to short-cut target group analysis, ignore the diversification implicit in a learner-centred approach and directly promote one of the many competing methods now 'on the market'. We felt it to be most important for teachers and planners to think first in terms of the needs, motivations and other relevant characteristics of their pupils and students, establish or negotiate worthwhile and feasible objectives, and then think how best to help the learners to achieve those objectives. In this view, decisions on methods and materials are highly contingent. Coste shows, however, that the various attempts to teach languages in a communicative perspective have much in common. In particular, the importance of the concept of autonomy to the fundamental aims of the Project has already been pointed out. The methodological implications of a

5

commitment to prepare students for autonomy are clearly far-reaching, as Holec shows in his contribution to this section.

Chapter Six deals with the question of evaluation and its role in communicative language learning systems development. An account is given by Trim of the principles which have underlain the work on evaluation, testing and assessment within the Project, dealing in turn with the questions: Why test? What to test? Who tests? and How to test? Oskarsson then presents a brief introduction to the notion of self-assessment – an indispensable tool for the promotion of learner autonomy – and makes detailed practical suggestions as to how it may be carried out.

Finally, in Chapter Seven, Edelhoff summarizes the implications of the approach for teacher training and sets out a programme for future work.

Appendix A gives the text of Recommendation R (82) 18 of the Committee of Ministers of the Council of Europe to member states concerning modern languages. Based on the work of Project 4, it sets down the steps recommended to be taken by member governments to promote the learning and teaching of modern languages for communication.

Appendix B lists the publications of the Council of Europe in the area covered by the Project.

J L M Trim   London, 1984

COUNCIL
OF EUROPE

CONSEIL
DE L' EUROPE

CHAPTER ONE:
A UNIT SCHEME

INTRODUCTION TO CHAPTER ONE

The first extract presents the framework in which the Modern Languages Project of the Council for Cultural Cooperation of the Council of Europe was carried out. In it, the Project Adviser, John Trim, describes the results of several years' reflection on the nature of the concept of 'unit', which was the key-concept in the description of the task originally given to the Project Group: 'examining the desirability and feasibility of developing a European unit/credit scheme for modern language learning by adults'.

If it was felt at first that this task implied the attempt to construct one single coherent overall system of learning-blocks, each of standardized content and size, it soon became apparent that such an approach would directly conflict with the overriding requirements of flexibility, differentiation and learner-centredness imposed by the infinite variety of individual and social conditions in the European area. The definition of 'unit' resulting from this reflection and presented in the extract is a far step from the original interpretation of the concept. It does not lead to the development of 'a European unit/credit system', but it provides the basis for the construction of a variety of unit-systems, designed in accordance with the specific conditions of each learning situation. It was for this reason that the first major publication of the Project Group, in 1973, was given the title of *Systems development in adult language learning*, where the plural-form *systems* is significant of the development in the Group's thinking since the beginning of the Project in 1971.

1. INTRODUCTION

The fundamental aim of the research and development programme under-taken by the group of experts called together in 1971 by the *Committee for Out-of-School Education and Cultural Development* of the *Council for Cultural Co-operation* (CCC) of the Council of Europe has been to create the conditions for the establishment of a suitable structural framework for the development, through international co-operation, of a coherent European policy in the field of adult language learning.

A European language policy of this kind should not simply accept and re-inforce existing structures and methods, but should be designed so as to serve the basic ideals of the CCC, such as:

a.   to facilitate the free movement of people and ideas in Europe by pro-viding the linguistic means for direct inter-personal communication;

b.   to make the process of language learning more democratic; by providing the conceptual tools for the planning, construction and conduct of courses closely geared to the needs, motivations and characteristics of learners and enabling them so far as possible to steer and control their own progress, we can encourage teachers and learners to take the deci-sions that directly affect them;

c.   to provide a framework for close and effective international co-operation in the organization of language learning, with the aim of placing at the disposal of adults a learner-centred, motivation-based language learning system designed to meet their diverse social and vocational needs.

From the beginning it was envisaged that this system might take the form of a "unit/credit scheme" ("*système d'unités capitalisables*"). Accordingly, one essential aim of the work of the group has been to examine the desirability and feasibility of developing a European unit/credit scheme for modern language learning by adults and, given that it is desirable and feasible, to formulate proposals for its introduction and implementation. In order to establish the desirability and feasibility of such a scheme, it is necessary to provide answers to a series of questions, such as:

1.   Can and should the global content of language learning be broken down into limited units, capable of being arranged in different ways to suit the needs of different groups of learners?

2.   Can learning objectives be specified in a sufficiently explicit way for the content of learning programmes to be assessed in unit/credit equiva-lences?

3.   Can learning systems be developed leading to the attainment of these objectives?

4.   Can the attainment of the objectives specified be reliably ascertained?

5.1. Does appropriate organizational and administrative machinery exist for the implementation of a unit/credit scheme?

5.2. If so, are the institutions concerned prepared to participate in the scheme?
5.3. If not, can the necessary machinery be established and made operational?
5.4. In that case, are member governments prepared to devote the necessary resources to its establishment?
5.5. If it were established, how would it relate to existing institutions in the field of adult language teaching and testing?

Of these questions, the most important, upon which all the rest depend, is undoubtedly the first, which has accordingly to be considered at some length.

2. LEARNING BY UNITS

Traditionally, language learning has been conceived as the steady progress of a learner from the condition of a "zero beginner" towards the virtually unattainable ideal of "native-like" proficiency. This progress is marked in a number of ways. There is a steady growth in the size of the vocabulary, the number of words and fixed idiomatic expressions available to the learner; a steady increase in his knowledge of morphological elements and categories as well as his ability to handle syntactic constructions of increasing complexity; a steady growth in the speed and efficiency of the encoding and decoding processes involved in the reception and production of speech and writing — increasing mastery, that is, of the skills of listening, speaking, reading and writing. As learning advances, progress is also marked by the learner's increasing "feel" for proper usage, both in matters of style and in finding the appropriate response to a given situation.

This conception of education inevitably evokes images of a journey or pilgrim's progress, a series of steps up a mountain, a straight and narrow path beset with difficulties and dangers, towards a distant goal which few but the truly devoted ever reach. However, the notion of a path, of steps, implies an ordering of the subject matter of any subject. Traditionally, again, this ordering has been based on a Euclidean analysis. From a small set of primitive definitions, axioms and postulates, complex concepts and propositions can be logically derived and used for the understanding and manipulation of natural phenomena of correspondingly increasing complexity.

The application of such a logical model to language learning is far from straightforward, since a natural language is not a strict logical system. However, classical language teaching seized upon those elements and aspects of language which could be treated in this way, and evolved a logico-developmental ordering starting with the simple sentence, in which, say, a singular 1st declension masculine noun in the nominative case was conjoined with a 1st conjugation verb in the 3rd person singular of the simple present tense. Steadily and systematically, other categories of number, case and gender, person, tense, mood and aspect were introduced, as well as other parts of speech with their morphological and syntactic properties. Each step increased the range and complexity of the sentences the learner was able to understand and compose.

Countless generations of school children have been taught Latin and Greek in this way in "grammar schools", by methods derived from the mediaeval *trivium* of grammar, logic and rhetoric. As the cultural and communicative functions of Latin and Ancient Greek faded, the educational value represented in their study became that of a "mental training" combining rote learning with an informal combinatory logic, as a way of selecting and grooming an intellectual elite. To this function, all other aspects of language were ruthlessly subordinated. Vocabulary was selected virtually at random, provided that it represented the desired conjugation or declension, or governed the desired case — or fell into a particularly favoured class of anomalous forms and exceptions to general rules. "The river having been crossed, the sailors were followed into the city by the camp-followers" might be followed immediately in the same set of exercises by: "the happiest man is he who exercises moderation in all things". The skills developed were those of a deciphering character on the receptive side, and of cautious, careful composition on the other. Avoidance of error was the first criterion of success, followed later by the achievement of elegance and precision of formulation. Spontaneity of expression and communicative effectiveness in social interaction did not arise in connection with a dead language and a dead culture and were neither cultivated nor esteemed. Thus early learning provides only intellectual satisfaction, and is not motivated by intrinsic usefulness or relevance to the learner's living situation. It is seen as a mere prolegomenon to later cultural studies which have inherent value.

By now the reader, though he may have recognized the picture painted above and experienced remembered pain or nostalgia in doing so, may wonder what the relevance can be to the issue of a unit/credit scheme for modern languages. In fact modern languages (as the name suggests) entered on the educational scene in the comparatively recent past as upstarts and poor relations of the much more prestigious classics. There are still to be found in positions of power and prestige in schools, and even more in universities, defenders of conservative principles, who are convinced that the maintenance of respectable academic and educational standards depends on the preservation of classical objectives, criteria and methods against the menace of meretricious banality and triviality.

Moreover, the modern movement itself, which in one way or another has been struggling for a century to liberate language study from its inherited burden of purism, elitist intellectualism and alienated formalism,[1] has for the most part preserved what might be called the Euclidean logico-developmental approach among its virtually unexamined presuppositions. The majority of courses, including those of an avowedly "communicative" character, continue to have a bony structure provided by the same notion of a defined step-by-step progress from the structurally simple to the structurally complex. Flesh is put upon these bones by demonstrating, usually through composed dialogues, how the structures being taught may be used in real-life situations. The lexicon is chosen partly so as to be useful in the situation portrayed, but also to contribute to a certain overall basic vocabulary and to provide suitable exponents for the structural categories that are the real substance of

---

[1] It has been represented to me that these lines, and this section more generally, are exaggerated and might easily alienate readers who might otherwise be convinced by the later argument. I am reluctant to remove them or tone them down because I know from personal experience that the views characterized here are more strongly entrenched than many may think and that those who hold them are deeply convinced that they are correct. Indeed, if there were not a good deal to be said in their favour they would not be so persistent or strongly held. The value of these objectives is, however, for the intellectual and cultural development of the very able, who are, alas, few in number. The conservative classicism I have described becomes, in my view, dangerous when it elevates the interests of the few above the many, despises or disregards the values of everyday life and everyday language, rejects social and linguistic change as degenerate, and is thus led to impose inappropriate objectives and methods on the majority of, especially, children, foredooming them to failure and rejection. "Meretricious banality and triviality" are equally real, complementary dangers. A continuing tension between these archetypal attitudes is probably inevitable and may be desirable, even creative.

the lesson. The learner's "educational biography" takes the form of a progress from one level to another, from "elementary" through "intermediate" to "advanced". Still far ahead lies the ideal of "native-like proficiency", which few believe can be attained within an educational framework.

The progress being smooth and continuous, "elementary", "intermediate" etc. do not constitute any natural levels which might serve as objectives for a learner. They are rather labels for certain periods of the learning process, vague and often highly arbitrary in character. What is regarded as "elementary" in one educational system may count as "advanced" in another — a fact which makes the establishment of equivalences across systems at once a difficult and delicate matter. In fact, it is the exigencies of the teaching system which determine the application of such labels rather than the needs of the learner or the nature of the language. A teaching institution offers classes of so many hours a week for so many weeks a year. The audience is often heterogeneous in character, and is often unable to contemplate very much self-study in a leisure activity. The successful course-writer or designer forecasts the language material that can be handled in that length of time, and the successful teacher organizes activities which will lead the majority of members of the class to master that material. The number and nature of the levels into which it segments the continuum of smooth progress are determined by such factors as the number of students, the number of years of study over which a viable audience can be maintained etc. The content of the language taught is determined by the text books used, examinations taken etc.

In small institutions, the number of classes will be small, and their membership heterogeneous. Very little sorting according to learner needs and characteristics is undertaken and a "highest common factor" principle will lead to generalized courses covering wide and overlapping bands of experience and ability as well as needs and motivations. Teachers, text book writers, course designers, and examining bodies are all likely to adapt to this situation if it is the predominant one. In particular, examinations will tend to be population-referenced and to rely upon continuity of experience to maintain a certain (inexplicit) standard and to develop testing techniques which emphasize reliability and distinguish well between candidates, producing a wide scatter of results along a continuum, a pass—fail threshold and perhaps some grade boundaries being imposed at some point or points along that continuum in accordance with past practice.

The educational structure and products which result are familiar to us all. Text books will have generalized titles like *Learning English, Le Français pour tous, Deutsch für Ausländer* and be subdivided into Book I, II, III etc. A teacher becomes used to distinguishing between students as being "better" or "worse", "faster" or "slower" learners, "more" or "less" gifted, of a "higher" or "lower" standard. When they are judged to be ready (or else as a matter of routine at the end of a particular stage of a course) students are entered for generalized proficiency examinations, which again are organized on a "straight-through" basis. Examinations are set at a series of levels, each more demanding in all respects than that next below. In an examination at any one level, candidates' performances are graded as "excellent", "very good", "fair", "poor" etc.

The image evoked, as we have seen, is that of a multitude of people setting out along a road. Some march briskly ahead, others drift along, or labour with dragging steps. Some walk a great distance, others stop after a few kilometres, from boredom or because the gradient steepens or because the end is nowhere in sight. But there is one way and all pass along it towards a single ultimate goal. Just as all children pass through recognizably similar stages as they move from their initial language-less state to possession of the knowledge and skills which enable any two adult members of a given language community to converse freely on all matters over the full range of public life and common experience even though they have never previously met.

This view of the organization of learning is of course by no means confined to languages. Organized education in almost all its branches has tended to proceed on the simple assumption that there exists a body of knowledge and skills to be acquired, constituting a "subject", and that learners vary primarily in their degree of success in mastering the subject. Hence the systems of levels and grades.

Given this approach, traditional examinations in languages have tended to be particularly inexplicit, relying on an intuitive consensus as to what kinds of linguistic texts ought to be within the compass of learners at different stages and the extent to which they should be able to handle them in different modes of activity. Since this consensus could not in the nature of things correspond to the intuitions of learners, the actual detailed content of language tests and examinations has been felt to be particularly arbitrary, even capricious, and has generated a good deal of anxiety among candidates, who have not known quite how to prepare themselves effectively.

In recent years, a good deal has been done, even within the limits of a monolithic approach, to make objectives more explicit. Proficiency scales have been set up, giving characteristic profiles of the kinds and levels of performance which can be expected of representative learners at different stages. Increasingly, these profiles have distinguished between the "4 skills" — listening, speaking, reading and writing.

Such scales are very useful, in at least three respects:

i.   The learner can compare his self-image with the stereotypes presented and roughly evaluate his own position;
ii. A framework is established on an operational basis providing a series of reference points within which a variety of different populations can be compared;
iii. The descriptions can give a rough characterization of the target audience to which learning materials of various kinds are addressed.

However, such scales have definite limitations:

1.   They tend to employ impressionistic evaluative terms to which no precise meaning can be given ("adequate", "good");

14

2. Some relational concepts are given a pseudo-absolute character ("intelligible", "comprehensible");
3. They tend to over-differentiate at low levels and under-differentiate at higher levels. Movement from one level to another is at first very rapid, whereas a proficient speaker may need years of experience to move from one higher level to another;
4. The lower levels tend to be defined in terms of incompetence, what a learner is unable to do, rather than what he can do;
5. At lower levels, limited knowledge and operational coverage is equated with unskilful and erratic performance. A student who learns to perform limited tasks to a high degree of efficiency cannot be properly located.

For these reasons, overall proficiency scales, though useful as tools for the rough sorting of populations are of limited value in setting learning objectives.

A more concrete approach to making learning objectives explicit has been through the development of "defined syllabuses". In these cases an attempt is made to set out explicitly what a learner should know and be able to do at a given stage. *Basic English* concentrated on a highly reduced lexicon, leaving syntax to the universal operations of the human mind and overlooking the often arbitrary and idiomatic nature of phrasal verbs (e.g. "put down" for "suppress"). Later specifications (*le Français fondamental,* the earlier *Volkshochschule Certificate* syllabuses, certain earlier Nuffield syllabuses) balanced the selection of vocabulary and sentence structures. They employed mainly criteria of frequency in vocabulary selection and of simplicity in selecting structures. They left aside questions of function and usage, and were concerned almost exclusively with early learning objectives (though supplementary lists of words and expressions for special purposes were also produced). From one point of view, the *Threshold Level* of the present project could be considered as an enrichment of this tradition by the introduction of systematically arranged notional and functional categories. That is probably the way that most outside observers and critics have seen it. In fact, however, though it owes much to the tradition outlined above, it derives from quite a different line of analysis.

The idea of language development as a straight-line process does not stand up to closer inspection. We are not all marching at different speeds along the same road towards a common goal. A more rewarding topographical, or geographical image can be derived from considering the way that the actual mobility of a human being develops. At first he crawls around a room, then a house, while pram tyre marks lead to the shops and the homes of his mother's friends and relations. Later, small footprints lead to the houses of his own friends, to school and gradually cover much of the home town. Later still, this network extends into a factory, an office, a shop, a university, and links up with other networks in other cities, other countries. In fact, this is no mere image. It is the matrix in which language is acquired and used. The overlapping networks of movement bring people into communicative confrontations, in which they create and re-create their relations and develop their language. In this way, as Hermann Paul pointed out a century ago, and successive generations of socio-linguists have rediscovered, every man forges

15

his own language. It is the density of overlapping communication networks that ensures social and linguistic cohesion.

The mature adult has learnt a complex body of social and linguistic rules which have made him a fully integrated member of a number of interlocking social groups. He knows how to behave with them, what to do and what to say, when, where, how and to whom. He can identify, understand and interpret what another member of one of these groups says to him. He has control over the transactional and interactional strategies which enable people to work together to common ends or to defend their own interests when purposes diverge. He is able, to a greater or lesser extent, to use his mother-tongue, developed and trained in the course of educational and professional experience, as a powerful intellectual tool. As he widens and extends the range and scope of his activities, and joins new social groups, he can rely on a very large area of overlap between his language and theirs (though there are always some adjustments to be made, some new language to be learnt) until this expansion crosses a linguistic frontier.

The position of an adult suddenly plunged into a foreign language environment is one of acute frustration. It is not quite true to say that he returns to an infant condition. Worse, he is an adult imprisoned within a baby. He already has the developed social skills, but cannot bring them into play. The young child, in a protected milieu, is gradually initiated into the life of the community and has to develop cognitive, social and linguistic systems in step with each other. As he does so, his immaturity is understood and tolerated, and social demands upon him grow as his competence grows. The adult finds himself confronted with a range of situations, which, despite all the knowledge and skill he has built up in his previous experience, he is incompetent to handle. It is a matter of urgency to him to become able to perform the tasks necessary to the mastering of those situations as soon as possible. The need becomes particularly urgent if the situations are problematic, if his intentions are liable to be thwarted and his well-being threatened.

Such situations may arise in a person's professional or working life; in his public life as he has to deal with authorities or with the general public, or transact the business of everyday practical living; in his social or private life, as he tries to make friends, to exchange information on a personal level, to recount experiences and describe places and things, to enter into emotional relationships with speakers of another language. The nature of the situations in which the need to communicate arises is a consequence and a part of the way of life of the person concerned. The demands made upon language and consequently the kind of language required to meet these demands vary as widely as do our different ways of life.

Seeing the role of language in adult life in this light gives a quite different perspective on language learning from the steady developmental progression envisaged in straight-through learning. In place of such generalized objectives as an "elementary", "intermediate" or "advanced" knowledge of a language, one looks to providing a learner with the body of knowledge and the skills he needs to solve a defined communication problem. These problems may be large or small. One may ask: *How do I buy a Metro ticket in Paris?* The answer may be given just by *un billet* or *un carnet*. Or one may ask: *How do I deal with public transport in France?* The answer will have to deal with all kinds of transport and cover enquiries about means of transport, fares, concessions, conditions, destinations, routes and connections, as well as the business of buying (or selling), boarding and leaving trains, explaining errors and loss of tickets etc. One may ask: *How do I cope with the business of everyday living as a visitor to a French-speaking country?* in which case the answer must cover not only travel but also shopping, eating out, accommodation, entertainment and cultural activities etc. It will be seen that each successive question is contained within the next. A simple-sounding question may evoke a simple-sounding answer: *How do I communicate with English people and cope with English life and culture? Speak English* — but what such deceptively simple global questions and answers mean emerges only as they are broken down into increasingly specific and concrete ones.

For a different way of life, we can expect a different set of questions: *How do I complain that my flat is damp? How do I deal with my landlord? How do I manage relations with authorities?* The same principles apply, but yield different answers.

This new perspective leads us to the central idea of learning by units: to organize specific learning programmes to serve particular defined purposes. We abandon the aim of leading the learner step-by-step along a path from the beginning to the end of a subject. Instead, we set out to identify a number of coherent but restricted goals relevant to the communicative needs of the learner. We then attempt to work out in detail the knowledge and skills which will equip the learner to use the language for the communicative purpose defined. In the light of his characteristics and resources we have then to establish a feasible learning programme leading to the mastery of this body of knowledge and skills, and means of testing and evaluation to provide feedback to all parties concerned as to the success of the programme.

Such a coherent language learning programme, leading to a defined communicative goal is a *unit*.[2]

---

[2] The reader may feel that the contrast between a linear learning programme and learning by units has been presented too much in terms of "black-and-white". After all experiences necessarily follow one another in time. There has to be an order of presentation and acquisition; surely it makes sense to arrange the order so as to make learning easier and more effective. Just so. As with all such questions, it is a matter of finding the right balance between complementary criteria. As language learners we have at the same time to be building up a set of responses to predictable situations and developing more general resources which enable us to respond to the unexpected. In schools we may be more concerned with long term objectives (though most children will also want to feel that they are learning something coherent and useful as they go along). Adults may have a more urgent short term need and no time to build up systematic knowledge over an extended period.

3. THE NATURE AND CONSTRUCTION OF UNITS

A major aspect of the work of the expert group since 1971 has been to establish the principles according to which units may be constructed.

The planning of a unit includes the following stages:

a. determine what the learner will need to *do* in using the language for communication in the real-life situations in which he is likely to be engaged;
b. calculate the knowledge and skills he will need to acquire in order to be able to act in the required way;
c. on this basis, set out clear, operational learning objectives;
d. assess the characteristics of the learner;
e. survey the resources of the teaching institution and the constraints under which it operates;
f. if necessary, modify objectives in the light of the analysis of resources;
g. plan the course, in terms of the activities required of the learner (including progression and phasing of objectives, methodology and roles of teacher and media);
h. conduct the course, with continuous monitoring of the learner's progress;
i. evaluate the learner's achievement and the effectiveness of the courses.

The procedure described above provides an adequate basis for the rationalization of decision-making. It examines the characteristics of all the components in the learning process, and their interaction, with particular attention to the interaction of the human participants, in the light of their needs, motivations, resources and responsibilities.

Language needs have been conceived by the group primarily in terms of the language-using operations in which the learner must participate effectively in order to communicate with members of the foreign language community concerned, for the purposes important to him in the light of his motivations. This does not mean that language learning is reduced to a practical training. Educational programmes have to take into account the development of the whole man, serving the personal and social development of the learner. A well-designed learning programme should render the learner not only able to communicate effectively. He should, along the way, have become more self-aware, more insightful into the problems of language and its use, more self-reliant and purposive as a learner, capable of continuing to learn independently. He should have learnt to co-operate with other members of a group. The recognition of these more general needs will have a profound influence on the methods to be used.

The motivations which impel a person to pursue a learning programme are complex. We may distinguish vocational, social and personal motivations, according to the aspect of the person's life concerned in relation to other people. In each case we may distinguish between satisfactions and expectations which may be functional, intellectual, emotional or material in character. We may further distinguish between intrinsic motivation (directly related to the accomplishment of the task set, for the purposes revealed by the needs analysis), and extrinsic motivation, where the satisfactions derived are irrelevant to the needs-related learning task — as for instance getting a rise in pay (vocational/material), enjoying the opportunity to meet people (social/emotional) or enjoying solving the puzzles set by translation (personal/intellectual).

The needs and motivations of the learner are important not only in determining the desirable objectives of his learning, but also in determining the amount of his own resources he is prepared to invest. How many hours a week is he prepared to devote to the task, and with what intensity of effort? Will he find the time and money for an intensive residential course? Will he buy course-books, tapes, dictionaries, a video-cassette recorder? It is not only the learner who must assess the priority to be given to investment in language learning in competition with other demands on his resources.[3] So must the teaching institutions, and also — perhaps less obviously — the various social agencies that support language-learning, whether by direct grants to students or by maintaining or financially supporting language teaching institutions. It is therefore necessary to take into account the needs, motivations, resources and responsibilities of these institutions — and the people who work in them — as well as of the society which maintains them, in order to arrive at a realistic language policy on a continental scale. This realism is not a mere acceptance of things as they are — planned international action is above all a force for change — but it serves to avoid an easy (but ultimately sterile) utopianism.

The acceptance of resources normally implies the acceptance of responsibilities for the effective deployment of those resources. In some cases, the necessary accounting can be carried out in strictly comparable financial terms. In the educational field, this form of accounting is rarely feasible or appropriate. In that case, it is understandable that society, and the institutions that act on its behalf, requires some form of publicly attested evaluation of the effectiveness of the learning processes in which it has invested its resources, as a mode of accountability and feed-back to the ultimate providers of resources to guide them in the difficult decisions they have to make in the allocation of resources. Naturally, the importance attached to such methods of feed-back will vary from one state to another. It is, however, a function of evaluation which should not be ignored.

Certain facts about units should be emphasized, most of which will be clear from the preceding discussion:

---

[3] The learner's resources include not only time, money and effort, but also less tangible things like study skills, memory and intelligence. A slower or "less able" learner will achieve less with the same expenditure of time, money and effort than a "gifted" learner because, in fact, his resources are more limited. Ability must obviously be taken into account in planning language programmes. However, the point of the argument here is to draw attention to factors usually less consciously attended to than "ability", which is often treated as if it were homogeneous and the only parameter to be taken into account.

i.   we do not arrive at units by subdividing a language, but by analyzing communicative needs;

ii.   there is no pre-ordained number of units for any language, but as many as will correspond to the communicative needs of different learner groups with defined objectives and worked-out learning programmes;

iii.   units are not of some standard size, but vary in magnitude according to the relative generality or specificity of the overall communicative goal (and, of course, the resources that make it feasible);

iv.   "communicative goals" are not restricted to conversation. All social uses of language, including the reading of scientific and technical literature or of literary texts, whether popular or classical, are communicative;

v.   the priority afforded to communicative goals does not exclude the development of units devoted to the consolidation of the learner's understanding and mastery of the formal linguistic system (e.g. grammar, intonation, phonetics) but such units should not predominate in such a way as to elevate intellectualized knowledge about the language above the ability to use it;

vi.   where learning is by units, a learning biography consists not of a straight-line progress from elementary to intermediate to advanced, but an accumulation of life-related learning experiences;

vii.   since, however (particularly if the units are, as they should if possible be, immediately use-related), each successive unit adds to the prior knowledge which is part of the learner's resources for tackling the next, a progression of some sort is established.

We are now in a position to give a reply to the first of our feasibility questions:

For adult learners with definable goals and limited time, it *is* desirable to break down the global objective of "learning a foreign language" into coherent, restricted learning units, and, by adopting an operational viewpoint, it is possible to do so in a principled way, defining the content of a unit in terms of:

a.   the situational structure of the social interactions in which the learner will characteristically be involved;

b.   the sequences of acts of speech (productive and receptive) necessary to effective participation in those social interactions;

c.   the communicative functions represented by the acts of speech;

d.   the notional and propositional content of the utterances necessary to communication in the given field of discourse;

e.   the linguistic expressions necessary to represent these functions and notions;

f.   the degrees of productive and receptive skill necessary to the performance of the acts of speech required to achieve the specified communicative interaction.

A model for the derivation and relation of these operational objectives was developed by K Bung and J L M Trim (doc. CCC/EES (73) 34 and 26) and applied to a restricted concrete case by K Bung (doc. CCC/EES (73) 16 rev.).

The model was then applied in thorough detail to one specified target audience by J van Ek in the CCC publication *The Threshold Level* (1975). Comparable definitions have since been drawn up for Spanish, German, Italian and Danish – in that order – and another is under way for Dutch. Furthermore, the model has been extended by adding an extensive classified inventory of categorized *actes de paroles* and a communicative grammar of French, which have been developed by a research team from CREDIF led by D Coste in collaboration with Professor E Roulet. From this extensive reservoir of materials, *Un Niveau-seuil*, specifications may be drawn for units at threshold level directed to the needs of diverse target audiences, taking into account the personalities of particular learners.

The multidimensional specification of the properties of utterances, on which the group's specification of objectives has been based, may be represented as a set of concentric discs, with the categories, sub-categories and exponents arranged on the rim (Fig. 1).

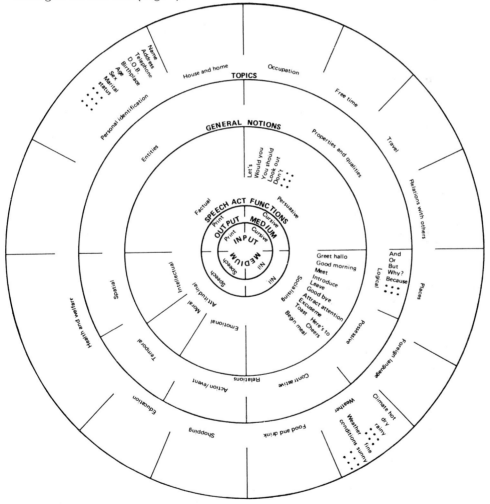

Figure 1

By revolving the discs relative to each other categories can be aligned in many different ways, so that each alignment specifies a particular utterance. By reference to such a diagram the categories relevant to the needs of a learner can be identified. Compatible alignments of the categories selected then characterize the universe of utterances which should be available to the learner. In many cases the linguistic exponents given for each category may be directly employed. However, the footnote by van Ek to page 72 of the *Threshold Level* should not be overlooked:

"It is clearly out of the question to draw up more or less complete lists of such exponents for all the notions listed in this study. Nor is it our aim to compose a phrase book. Using language creatively is part of everyday speech, even at low levels of proficiency. At T-Level a learner who has at his disposal 'where' (deixis: place), the verbal phrase 'to be born', the pronoun 'you' (deixis), and some basic grammatical rules, has the ability to inquire after a person's birthplace, even without having learnt the exponent 'where were you born?' by heart."

4. THE FRAMEWORK OF A UNIT/CREDIT SYSTEM

A European unit/credit scheme, at any rate in the field of language learning, must provide a flexible framework for the fully participatory development of language learning systems appropriate to different learning situations at different times and places.

It is neither feasible, nor desirable, for the expert group to attempt to define, once and for all, a canonical set of language learning objectives. It is not possible to foresee the needs of all audiences or the characteristics of all learning situations. Such a scheme would inevitably be subject-based rather than learner-centred and be in grave danger of imposing oppressive constraints on the development of rationalized language learning.

What is required is a flexible, supportive structure which will enable the decisions on the objectives and methods of language learning to be decentralized, made on each occasion by the parties involved in the light of their understanding of the particular circumstances, especially the needs and characteristics of the learners concerned.

There is no intention on the part of the group to dictate a single objective or set of objectives to the language learning world at large. The extent to which it will be feasible to make unique systems for unique groups, however, will depend on the resources of time and skill available to them in relation to those of money and things. Effective learner autonomy is a highly desirable educational objective. On the other hand, if democratic procedures are ineffective, the dangers of disillusion and loss of self-confidence are all too apparent. The less experienced the learners and teachers concerned, the more support they will require. More decisions may have to be made by syllabus designers and course writers, so that the energies of teachers and learners may be concentrated on the act of learning itself rather than on the prolegomena. What planning decisions and choices are made must be prepared with clarity and explicitness.

It is well-known that the learning population is pyramidal in shape, if length of study (or height of attainment) are plotted against numbers. Inversely, later stages of language learning are normally more specialized. As opposed to early learning, where common objectives (common functions and notions, major grammatical categories, structures and rules, generic terms and other high-frequency lexicon) are dominant, and progress in general proficiency is rapid, later learning brings increased manipulative skill, accessions to vocabulary in specific topic areas dependent on the specific nature of experience, more effective performance of relevant functions. But in the same way that inflating a balloon with a steady stream of air brings a slower and slower increase in its diameter, a given amount of learning effort produces less and less in the way of a general rise in proficiency level as learning proceeds. From "zero beginner" to "waystage" may require, say, a year's work in a multimedia extensive framework. From basic professional competence to native-like proficiency may represent many years of intensive professional work — and may still be inadequate for special purposes. We thus have two inversely related curves (Fig. 2):

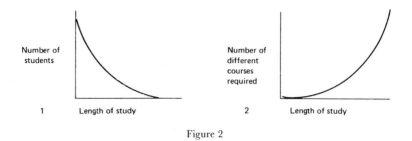

Figure 2

Their combination produces on the one hand a small number of learning programmes with little differentiation for large numbers of early learners, on the other hand a large number of highly differentiated learning programmes for small numbers of more advanced learners. The effect may be combined with the "disc" representation of multi-dimensional objectives to form an inverted, truncated cone (Fig. 3(a)). The vertical axis of the central be-

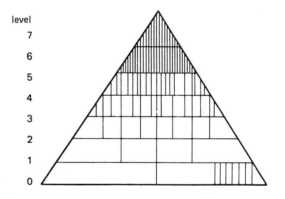

Figure 3(a) Diagram to show diminishing size of audience and proliferation of differentiated courses with increasing study time and level of proficiency

havioural spindle may be taken to represent increasing manipulative skill in the processing of language as input and output — though we must remember that the various sub-processes involved do not always develop at the same rate either as each other or as the growth in knowledge of content. The vertical axis in respect of functions indicates an increasing refinement of functions, reflected in a more delicate sub-classification, the greater use of indirect speech-acts, more combinations of functions in simple utterances and the wider choice of exponents appropriate to different situations. The vertical axis in the case of general notions will similarly represent increasingly fine semantic differentiation of entities, qualities and relations and greater power in their combination. In the case of topics, we may have an indefinite growth in the number of topics handled (though a hierarchical ranking of topics is contentious) and in the distinction of sub-topics and associated specific notions, as well as in the associated, largely concrete and particularistic vocabulary. Taking these together the diagram appears as follows (Fig. 3(b)).

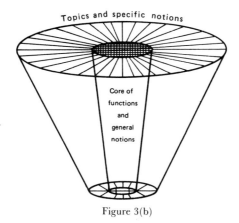

Figure 3(b)

Language learning will then represent a vertical and horizontal expansion within the space thus defined, in a way related to the patterns of communication in which the learner is involved, or expects to be involved.

Mass learning objectives invite the investment of large resources in order to achieve economies of scale and produce a very low *per capita* cost. Specialized, or higher level objectives for small numbers of learners invite ways of reducing the inherently high *per capita* costs by pooling resources and increasing the size of the dispersed audience. Market forces tend towards a rationalization of provision, but rather erratically. Thus the market for generalized beginners' English swarms with overlapping and competing courses. New ones appear continuously and are subject to strong selection pressures. This area is accordingly lively and innovative. A single acceptable advanced special purpose course, on the other hand, may satiate the market for a long period and exert a conservative influence. In fact, courses for special purposes are often produced within teaching institutions as by-products of teaching activity. They are thus likely to be produced by isolated workers and thus to be dependent upon their own mode of use and methods of teaching. In many cases they are unknown outside the institutions and are difficult to publish onto an unknown market. Even if other institutions are invited to take up such a course, it may not fit into their institutional structure. If teaching in that area is not available, the materials may be usable only in an extreme form of self-instruction (the learner being left to get on with it by himself) for which it has not been planned or intended.

There is thus scope for co-operation on a national and international scale between related institutions. This would include: those involved in large-scale multimedia learning systems; those concerned with closely related specialized language learning areas for relatively small numbers. The expert group can act as a focus and "hold the ring" for the interaction of such groups of institutions, which would apply its principles or even produce a unit/credit system in a given area. Examples might be: (a) industrial in-service training; (b) training for international administration; (c) language training for immigrants.

The degree of explicitness in the specification of objectives mentioned above appears to be sufficient for it to be possible to establish a system of equivalences between distinct objectives specified according to the same principles, thus providing the basis for unit/credit ratings.

COUNCIL
OF EUROPE

CONSEIL
DE L' EUROPE

2   CHAPTER TWO: 2

NEEDS

INTRODUCTION TO CHAPTER TWO

From the start of the Modern Languages Project it was recognized that if language learning was to be truly efficient and effective it would have to be geared, as directly as possible, to satisfying the needs of the learners. The analysis – or, as it came to be called later on, the identification – of foreign-language needs thus became one of the main areas of investigation. The term 'analysis' was replaced by 'identification' when it became clear that 'finding out about needs' was not simply a matter of applying a rigorous scientific procedure, by means of which a person's 'needs' could be determined once and for all. On the contrary, it was recognized that a large variety of methods might suit the even much larger variety of conditions – and, it should be added, the variety of purposes for which insight into needs might be required – and that a person's needs – like his personality – are subject to constant change and development, also – and perhaps even especially – during a learning process. Finally, it became clear that since language learning is invariably part of a person's overall development, the determination of language-learning needs should be related to more comprehensive developmental needs.

The extracts selected for this chapter present an overview of the more fundamental work on 'needs' carried out in the framework of the Modern Languages Project. In the first extract René Richterich, who was involved in this aspect of the Project from the beginning, succinctly describes the nature, roles and possible forms of the identification of needs. The second extract presents a detailed analysis and classification of major aspects of the identification of the needs of adult learners. It forms part of a study by Richterich and Chancerel, *Identifying the needs of adults learning a foreign language*, which, since its first appearance in 1977, has found practical application in numerous projects connected or unconnected with the Modern Languages Project, both in and outside Europe. The third extract, from a paper read by Jan van Ek in 1981 at a modern language teachers' conference in Milan, deals comprehensively with foreign-language learning needs of children and adolescents in general education, relating these needs to more general learning needs. The paper owes a good deal to Louis Porcher's *Interrogations sur les besoins langagiers en contextes scolaires*, published by the Council of Europe in 1980.

from R Richterich in: *A European unit/credit system for modern language learning by adults.*

IDENTIFYING LANGUAGE NEEDS AS A MEANS OF DETERMINING EDUCATIONAL OBJECTIVES WITH THE LEARNERS

In this introductory statement I propose to ask a few fundamental questions; I shall then give one or more possible answers to them – and possible is the important word here – which we can subsequently go into in more detail, discuss and complete in order, finally, to select one or several possible approaches to the task of defining the functions of the identification of language needs when setting up unit/credit systems for the learning of modern languages. This statement should be directly related to the study entitled: 'Identifying the needs of adults learning a foreign language (Collection of information for use in determining learner needs in a European unit/credit system for adult language learning.)' (R Richterich, J L Chancerel).

First question: What is an identification of language needs?

Possible reply: It is the compilation, treatment and exploitation for heuristic and didactic purposes, of certain information about an individual, group of individuals, institution, or society, in relation to the actual or intended use and teaching/learning of a particular language.

Comments

1. I have chosen the word *identification* rather than the more frequently employed term *analysis* in order to dispel the idea that the discovery of language needs is a matter for specialists using scientific techniques which are complex and hard to manipulate. We shall see, on the contrary, that an identification can be made at different levels of analysis, by different types of persons, with the help of a large number of techniques, for different purposes and at different times.

2. The concept of a need is still ambiguous, especially as it is used in the didactics of languages. Although this is not the place to go into the subtleties of definition and interpretation, three things should be pointed out:

a. A need does not exist independent of a person. It is people who build their own images of their needs on the basis of data relating to themselves and their environment which give them an awareness of a certain lack;

b. Nor does a need exist without a second awareness, namely that there is some means of satisfying it.

c. The need can be satisfied only by recourse to an element external to the person.

3. In the didactics of languages the concept of a need is of use to us only in so far as it enables individuals and institutions, working from information relating to it, to define their learning objectives more clearly.

4. For us, needs and objectives are two concepts which do not merge into one, as is often the case, but remain parallel and indissociable. Let us say, to simplify matters, that objectives are the explicit translation in pedagogical terms of information of different types derived from individuals and institutions – a body of particulars which, when combined, will produce what Rousson calls a project, realistic or not, explicit or impicit, individual or collective, and which represents the needs.

5. As a need cannot exist without an awareness that there is some means of satisfying it, so an objective cannot be defined without a realization that there are means of achieving it and ascertaining whether it has been achieved.

6. Essentially, therefore, an identification of language needs is an heuristic device conducive to the realization by individuals and institutions of factors which can affect the learning/teaching of a foreign language and by means of which it is possible to define learning objectives explicitly.

Second question: Why is it necessary to identify language needs?

Possible reply: In order to become aware of the learning conditions of individuals or groups and to align these with their physical, intellectual and emotional possibilities, as well as to devise learning materials which will approach the real use made of the language taught; thus, to define pedagogical objectives through negotiation with the learners.

Comments

1. The achievement of a learning objective, like the satisfaction of a need, implies a search for a compromise between the learner and an educational institution. The starting point for that research should be a better knowledge of the possibilities and resources of both parties.

2. In learner-centred language-learning systems the final object and culmination of the identification of language needs will be the definition of objectives and choice of means of achieving them, which will take place through negotiations with the learners.

3. This implies that the training institutions will possess flexible structures for reception and administrative and educational organization, so that individual language needs really can be taken into account.

4. If we accept that the purpose of an identification of language needs is, by compiling information about and with the learners, to define objectives with them and offer them learning conditions and contents more nearly suited to their possibilities and expectations, then the success of this project will depend upon several factors, such as:

Who identifies the needs?

What sources of information are available?

What resources in time, money and staff can be called upon?

When does the identification take place?

Where?

Thus it can take place at different levels and with differing intermediary goals.

Third question: Who can identify language needs, and how?

Possible reply: Anybody, and in various ways, depending upon the type of information which it is thought necessary to obtain and the level of awareness which it is desired to produce.

Comments

1. First of all, certain distinctions should be made:

a.   An identification of language needs can be made before and/or after learning a language.

b.   The information compiled can be comprehensive or particular, general or specific.

c.   The identification of language needs may take place in different types of situations and be performed by different agencies:

i.   one person alone,

ii.   a person with one other person,

iii.   a group,

iv.   a person with one person representing an institution (for education or use, or an institution specializing in sociological analyses),

v.   a person with several others representing one institution,

vi.   a person with several others representing different types of institutions,

vii.   a group with one person representing an institution,

viii.   a group with several others representing one institution,

ix.   a group with several others representing different types of institutions.

d.   The identification of language needs may require the production of information relating to different contents:

i.   learning conditions for a particular language,

ii.   learning content,

iii.   conditions of actual use of a given language,

iv.   contents of actual use of a given language.

2. It is clear that although the ultimate purpose of an identification of language needs is always the same, the forms it may take, the persons who may be involved in it and the methods which may be employed can all differ. For example:

a.   A future learner makes an initial identification of his language needs simply by reading the prospectuses of different educational establishments, becoming acquainted with their requirements and learning conditions and then selecting the one which seems best to suit the objectives which he has very indistinctly formulated in the mere act of reading the prospectuses.

b.   The same future learner may identify his language needs in somewhat greater detail if he gets in touch with an educational establishment and asks for particulars from a secretary or has an interview with an educational adviser or the director.

c.   But an educational establishment may also have a guidance service which will provide specialized staff to identify the future learner's language needs using a range of techniques such as interviews, questionnaires, language tests and

31

attitude scales, and to define his objectives with him and advise him in choosing the means of achieving them.

d. By structured group interviews at the beginning of the learning process, a teacher can try to identify certain general needs of the learners and can teach them to decide upon their pedagogical objectives.

e. He can repeat this operation several times during the learning process, achieving increasingly elaborate discussions, negotiations and decisions in the language being taught.

f. Questionnaires, tests and attitude scales may be incorporated into the educational material, enabling the learner to see from time to time where he stands in terms of his level of attainment, in relation to his own image of his needs and objectives.

g. An educational establishment may carry out an identification of the language needs of a specific population by means of surveys and enquiries conducted by specialized staffs, so that it may offer learning conditions corresponding to the demands of that population.

h. An institution in which a language is used may employ specialists to determine, by means of observation, questionnaires, interviews and content analyses, how the language is used in its various activities, in order to propose learning contents to educational establishments which correspond to its linguistic reality.

3. These are only a few examples which should show the diversity of forms, means and persons which may be involved in an identification of language needs.

Conclusions

One would certainly not wish to contest the essential value of enquiries and analyses of language needs carried out on a large scale using established methods of investigation. Any study which can help us to a better knowledge of the processes by which a foreign language is learned, and its actual operation and use outside the learning situation, is indispensable. I believe, however, that the identification of language needs may be conceived in other terms as well, particularly in relation to its immediate use in teaching/learning. In this sense,

– it will not be performed by specialists only, but by anyone concerned in the learning/teaching of a foreign language;
– it may lead to a new awareness at different levels of precision, none being favoured *a priori*;
– it may be carried out at different times and using a wide range of methods;
– it will become a tool serving the learners, teachers and institutions in defining their objectives more clearly and selecting the learning conditions and contents through which they may be achieved;
– it may become a factor in the negotiation of the compromises which are inevitable in any achievement of objectives and satisfaction of needs;
– it may be incorporated into the pedagogical material and thereby become an heuristic and didactic resource;
– above all, it does not fit into any pre-established model for every person or group or institution can identify their language needs to the extent to which they need to be aware of them.

from: R Richterich and J-L Chancerel, *Identifying the needs of adults learning a foreign language*

TYPES OF INFORMATION

5. IDENTIFICATION BY THE LEARNER OF HIS NEEDS

I. Identification by the learner of his needs in relation to his resources

I.B Before the course

When a person wishes to learn a foreign language, has decided to or is about to start doing so, it is advisable that he himself should form an idea of the amount of time and money at his disposal and the place where the learning might be done.

In the main the choice of the type of instruction and teaching establishment will depend on these three factors. Besides this, certain details about his identity are invariably essential. But the future learner should also become aware of certain characteristics of his own personality that may play an important part in determining his behaviour and methods of learning.

Most of this information can be compiled by the learner himself without any need for using complicated methods; nevertheless, it might be advisable for him to consult a teaching establishment or advisory service, especially with regard to the becoming aware of his personality. It is possible also that the material required to help the potential learner to collect this sort of information could be made available to him through teaching systems so as to enable him to make his decisions with full knowledge of all the facts. At the present time this is generally done by means of written or visual advertisements or by word of mouth.

Types of information

T.1. Learner's identity

T.1.1.	Age
T.1.2.	Sex
T.1.3.	Marital status
T.1.4.	Number of children
T.1.5.	Nationality
T.1.6.	Address
T.1.7.	Religion
T.1.8.	Number of brothers and sisters
T.1.9.	Occupation of father and mother
T.1.10.	Schooling – General, vocational, specialized (number of years)
T.1.11.	Certificates and diplomas
T.1.12.	Present occupation (eg engineer)
T.1.13.	Present position (eg sales manager)
T.1.14.	Previous occupations

T.1.15.   Previous positions held
T.1.16.   Place of work
T.1.16.1. Geographical location
T.1.16.2. Type of firm
T.1.17.   Leisure-time pursuits and hobbies
T.1.18.   Outside activities (politics, arts, clubs, etc)

T.2. Learner's personality
T.2.1.   Personality traits (reserved/frank, timid/venturesome, introvert/extrovert, trusting/suspicious, etc)
T.2.2.   Capability (intelligence, memory, ability to learn, etc)
T.2.3.   Attitude (positive/negative to language learning in general, to a particular language, to its culture, to its civilization, to the people speaking it, etc)

T.3.   Time at learner's disposal
T.3.1.   Number of hours a day
T.3.2.   Number of hours a week
T.3.3.   Number of weeks a month
T.3.4.   Number of months a year
T.3.5.   Number of years
T.3.6.   At what time of day?
T.3.7.   On which days of the week?
T.3.8.   At what time in private life (holidays, free time)?
T.3.9.   At what time in working life (during working hours, free time)?
T.3.10. Learning during working hours
T.3.11. Learning outside working hours

T.4.   Where learning is done
T.4.1.   In the place where the learner lives
T.4.2.   In a place near where he lives
T.4.3.   In another place but in the same country
T.4.4.   In a country where the language is spoken
T.4.5.   In a teaching establishment
T.4.6.   At the place of work
T.4.7.   Near the place of work
T.4.8.   At home

T.5.   Financing of tuition
T.5.1.   Paid leave from work
T.5.2.   Partially paid leave from work
T.5.3.   Unpaid leave from work
T.5.4.   All tuition paid for by the establishment where the future learner will use his knowledge
T.5.5.   Tuition partly paid for by the establishment where the future learner will use his knowledge
T.5.6.   Tuition paid for entirely by the future learner
T.5.7.   Tuition paid for entirely by a third party (eg parents)
T.5.8.   Tuiton paid for partly by a third party
T.5.9.   Cost of tuition
T.5.9.1. Course fee

T.5.9.2. Materials and equipment
T.5.9.3. Travelling expenses
T.5.9.4. Cost of board
T.5.9.5. Pocket money
T.5.9.6. Loss of wages
T.5.10. Need to obtain a loan
T.5.11. Possibility of obtaining a grant

Possible steps to be taken by the learner
S.1. Consulting a person who has had experience of a given type of course
S.2. Consulting a person who has had experience of learning modern languages
S.3. Paying attention to the publicity materials of teaching establishments
S.4. Consulting one or more teaching establishment
S.5. Consulting an advisory service
S.6. Consulting third parties (eg parents)
S.7. Consulting the personnel department of an establishment where the knowledge is to be used
S.8. Consulting superiors at an establishment where the knowledge is to be used

Means of obtaining information
M.1. Questionnaires
M.2. Personality tests
M.3. Aptitude tests
M.4. Attitude scales
M.5. Interviews

I.D During the course

The information the learner has obtained and the ideas he has formed concerning his resources before starting to learn a language will be compared by him, whilst the course continues, with any changes that may take place in his identity and personality, his available time and money and his opportunities for travel. Some of these changes may have a decisive influence on the continuation of his course and cause him to make other decisions than the original ones. Discussion and negotiation will then have to be entered into with the teaching establishment to find out what are the possibilities for adaptation and for arriving at fresh compromises. If the learner is able to obtain most of this information himself, it may be that the teaching material itself will provide him with some of the means for doing so and that the establishment will look into the question of resources with him periodically.

Types of information

T.1. Learner's identity

Have there been any changes likely to affect the course?

T.1.1. Marital status
T.1.2. Address
T.1.3. Present occupation
T.1.4. Present position held
T.1.5. Place of work
T.1.6. Leisure-time pursuits and hobbies
T.1.7. Outside activities

Is the information regarding his personality confirmed and what is its influence on the course?

T.2.1. Personality traits
T.2.2. Capability
T.2.3. Attitude

T.3. Time at learner's disposal

Is the amount of time available still the same?

T.3.1.
    to   *cf* I.B, T.3.
T.3.14.

T.4. Where learning is done

Is there any reason to change the place?

T.4.1.
    to   *cf* I.B, T.4.
T.4.7.

T.5. Financing of tuition

Are his financial resources still the same?

T.5.1.
    to   *cf* I.B, T.5.
T.5.11.

Possible steps to be taken by the learner

S.1. Negotiations with teaching establishment
S.2. Negotiations with personnel department of the establishment where the knowledge is to be used
S.3. Negotiations with the superiors at an establishment where the knowledge is to be used
S.4. Negotiations with a third party

Means of obtaining information

M.1. Questionnaires
M.2. Personality tests
M.3. Aptitude tests
M.4. Attitude scales
M.5. Interviews

II. Identification by the learner of his needs in relation to his objectives

II.B Before the course

In most cases the future learner has only a very vague idea of the objectives he would like to achieve by learning a foreign language and, above all, he is unable to specify them. However, this should not prevent him from realizing just how precisely he is capable of thinking out those objectives and then asking himself questions about the spheres in which he proposes to use the second language, the types of use he envisages and the skills he will need to acquire. Even if his description of his objectives does not get beyond nebulous fancies and vague plans, it will nevertheless play an important part in the choice of a course. Here too the future learner ought to be assisted by the provision of means enabling him to become more aware, which is intimately and directly related to the identification of needs in relation to resources and to methods of assessment.

Types of information

T.1.   Level of description of objectives

T.1.1.   In general terms
T.1.2.   In exact operational terms

T.2.   Areas in which the language is intended to be used

T.2.1.   Working life
T.2.2.   Private life (social contacts, cultural interests, etc)

T.3.   Ways in which the language is intended to be used

T.3.1.   Language activities (eg telephoning, negotiating, writing letters)
T.3.2.   Language functions (eg asking for information, giving orders, arguing, explaining)
T.3.3.   Language situations (eg face to face, in a working group)
T.3.4.   Referential objects (eg everyday communications, scientific references)

T.4.   Language skills to be developed

T.4.1.   Understanding speech
T.4.2.   Understanding written matter
T.4.3.   Speaking
T.4.4.   Writing

Possible steps to be taken by the learner

S.1.   Consulting prospectuses issued by teaching establishments
S.2.   Consulting the syllabuses of teaching establishments
S.3.   Consulting lists of objectives prepared in advance
S.4.   Applying to one or more teaching establishments
S.5.   Applying to an advisory service

Means of obtaining information

M.1.   Questionnaires
M.2.   Interviews
M.3.   Lists of language activities, functions and situations prepared in advance

II.D During the course

It may be supposed that the learner's vague ideas about his objectives will alter and become clearer as the course proceeds. The very fact of learning a modern language will, indirectly, alter his first idea. But the teaching establishment will be able to give him direct assistance in appreciating such changes by incorporating in its instructional material instruments enabling the learner to describe ever more clearly the aims of each unit of learning. This means that the teacher must have the professional skill and institutional facilities for taking these changes into consideration and adapting his teaching accordingly.

Types of information

T.1.   Level of description of objectives

T.1.1.   Long-term objectives
T.1.1.1.   General objectives
T.1.1.2.   Operational objectives
T.1.2.   Short-term objectives
T.1.2.1.   General objectives
T.1.2.2.   Operational objectives

T.2.   Changes in areas in which the language is intended to be used

cf II.B, T.2.

T.3.   Changes in ways in which the language is intended to be used

cf II.B, T.3.

T.4.   Changes in language skills to be developed

cf II.B, T.4.

Possible steps to be taken by the learner

S.1.   Learning to define learning objectives
S.2.   Agreeing the necessary adaptations with teacher and teaching establishment

Means of obtaining information

M.1.   Questionnaires
M.2.   Interviews
M.3.   Lists of language activities, functions and situations prepared in advance
M.4.   Methods of defining objectives

III. Identification by the learner of his needs in relation to methods of assessment

III.B Before the course

Definition of objectives and definition of the methods of checking and assessing how they are to be attained cannot be separated. The future learner will first take into account the information given in his language background and try to evaluate his previous knowledge of the language he intends to learn. Even if this assessment is vague and subjective, it is nonetheless important since it reflects his idea of what he has accomplished, an idea that it is essential to know about because it will persist throughout the course. The next essential is for the future learner to decide what sort of qualification he wishes or is required to obtain.

Types of information

T.1. Learner's language background

T.1.1.	Native tongue(s)
T.1.2.	Father's native tongue(s)
T.1.3.	Mother's native tongue(s)
T.1.4.	Foreign languages known
T.1.5.	Foreign languages learnt
T.1.6.	Time when languages were learnt
T.1.6.1.	Before schooldays
T.1.6.2.	At school
T.1.6.3.	After completion of schooling
T.1.7.	Length of this course
T.1.7.1.	Number of weeks, months or years
T.1.7.2.	Number of hours a week
T.1.7.3.	How long is it since the learner was last learning a language?
T.1.8.	Types of courses
T.1.8.1.	Language courses without audio-visual aids or language laboratory
T.1.8.2.	Audio-visual language courses with language laboratory
T.1.8.3.	Audio-visual language courses without language laboratory
T.1.8.4.	Individual study without any particular method
T.1.8.5.	Individual study by self-tuition method
T.1.8.6.	Radio or television language courses
T.1.8.7.	Crash course
T.1.8.8.	Suggestopaedia
T.1.8.9.	Large group (over ten learners)
T.1.8.10	Small group (less than ten learners)
T.1.9.	Where learning is done
T.1.9.1.	Compulsory school
T.1.9.2.	Vocational school
T.1.9.3.	University
T.1.9.4.	Language centre attached to a university
T.1.9.5.	School specializing in teaching foreign languages
T.1.9.6.	Training centre run by a firm or other institution needing language knowledge
T.1.9.7.	Official or semi-official permanent education establishment
T.1.9.8.	Outside the country where the language is spoken
T.1.9.9.	In the country where the language is spoken
T.1.9.10	At home
T.1.10.	Types of qualification obtained for languages learnt
T.1.11.	Use made of languages learnt
T.1.11.1.	Oral

T.1.11.1.1.   Frequently
T.1.11.1.2.   Occasionally
T.1.11.1.3.   Never
T.1.11.2.   Written
T.1.11.2.1.   Frequently
T.1.11.2.2.   Occasionally
T.1.11.2.3.   Never
T.1.11.3.   In working and public life
T.1.11.4.   In private life
T.1.11.5.   In the country where the language is spoken
T.1.11.6.   Outside the country where the language is spoken
T.1.12.   Courses at present being taken in one or more languages besides the one contemplated
T.1.12.1.   Length of course(s)
T.1.12.2.   Type of course
T.1.12.3.   Where course(s) is/are being taken

T.2.   Assessment of level attained in language contemplated

T.2.1.   Understanding of speech
T.2.2.   Understanding of writing
T.2.3.   Speaking
T.2.4.   Writing

T.3.   Type of qualifications aimed at

T.3.1.   Diploma of an official establishment
T.3.2.   Diploma of a semi-official establishment
T.3.3.   Diploma of a non-official establishment
T.3.4.   Testimonial
T.3.5.   Certificate
T.3.6.   None

T.4.   Purpose of qualification aimed at

T.4.1.   Professional or vocational
T.4.2.   Cultural

Possible steps to be taken by the learner

S.1.   Compilation of data on his own language background
S.2.   Obtaining information on types of qualification available
S.3.   Getting information on requirements for obtaining the various types of qualification
S.4.   Applying to one or more teaching establishments
S.5.   Applying to an advisory service
S.6.   Applying to someone with experience of assessment problems

Means of obtaining information

M.1.   Questionnaires
M.2.   Placement tests
M.3.   Aptitude tests

III.D During the course

Throughout the whole of his course, the learner ought to be able to check his progress and compare his newly acquired knowledge with his ideas concerning his previous knowledge. Constant encouragement of this kind is recognized as an important factor in motivation. The terms and content of such continuous assessment and the conditions for obtaining a final qualification should be defined jointly with his teacher and the teaching establishment. Just as with the specification of objectives, assessment should be an integral part of the learning material and should be carried out at two levels – general and operational. This will also help the learner to appreciate his own strategies.

Types of information

T.1.   Conditions of assessment

T.1.1.   Objective assessment from outside
T.1.2.   Subjective assessment from outside
T.1.3.   Guided self-assessment
T.1.4.   Subjective self-assessment
T.1.5.   Continuous assessment
T.1.6.   Periodical assessment
T.1.7.   Single assessment
T.1.8.   Individual assessment
T.1.9.   Assessment in groups
T.1.10.   Assessment criteria
T.1.10.1.   Marks
T.1.10.2.   Appraisal of general progress

T.2.   Types of assessment

T.2.1.   Objective tests
T.2.2.   Self-assessment
T.2.3.   Check exercises
T.2.4.   Homework
T.2.5.   Examinations
T.2.6.   Alternation of educational assessment and actual use of the language

T.3.   Level of assessment

T.3.1.   Assessment of general objectives
T.3.2.   Assessment of operational objectives

T.4.   Content of assessment

T.4.1.   Phonetics
T.4.2.   Morphology
T.4.3.   Syntax
T.4.4.   Lexis
T.4.5.   Language activities
T.4.6.   Language functions
T.4.7.   Language situations
T.4.8.   Referential objects
T.4.9.   Understanding of speech

T.4.10. Understanding of written matter
T.4.11. Speaking
T.4.12. Writing
T.4.13. General content (eg textbooks, methods, threshold-levels).

Possible steps to be taken by the learner

S.1. Self-observation during course
S.2. Becoming aware of own learning strategies
S.3. Discussion of methods of assessment with teacher and teaching establishment

Means of obtaining information

M.1. Progress tests
M.2. Examination tests
M.3. Self-assessment

IV. Identification by the learner of his needs in relation to curricula

IV.B Before the course

The future learner will have chosen his course in accordance with his resources, his more or less clearly defined objectives and the methods of assessment he would like to have applied to him. The more information on these three matters he has collected, the clearer will be his awareness of his needs and the better able he will be to make his choice. In order that systems really centred on the learner may operate properly, it seems that neutral advisory services should be set up whose role would be to help the learner obtain information about his needs and to advise him about possible courses. At the present time it appears that he relies too much on the publicity materials of teaching establishments and his impression of how good they are.

It should be remembered that a teaching syllabus represents the implementation of means available for the attainment of objectives fixed by reference to methods of assessment and resources. The idea formed by a future learner will therefore depend on the information he has previously obtained.

Types of information

T.1. Types of establishment

cf V.B, T.1.

T.2. Time taken up by the syllabus

T.2.1. Number of hours a day
T.2.2. Number of days a week
T.2.3. Number of weeks a month
T.2.4. Number of months a year
T.2.5. Number of years
T.2.6. At what time of day

T.2.7. On which days in the week
T.2.8. During holidays

T.3. Where learning is done

cf I.B, T.4.

T.4. Cost of course

T.4.1. Enrolment fee
T.4.2. Cost of course
T.4.3. Cost of materials
T.4.4. Cost of board
T.4.5. Pocket money

T.5. Teacher

T.5.1. Image of teacher
T.5.2. Desired relationship between teacher and learner

T.6. Learners

T.6.1. Number of learners in group
T.6.2. Self-tuition
T.6.3. Desired relationship between learners

T.7. Technical aids to learning

T.7.1. Language laboratory
T.7.2. Television
T.7.3. Radio
T.7.4. Audio-visual aids
T.7.5. Visual aids
T.7.6. Auditive aids
T.7.7. Printed aids
T.7.8. Multi-media

T.8. Areas in which curriculum is used

T.8.1. Working life
T.8.2. Private life

T.9. Content of syllabus

T.9.1. Phonetics
T.9.2. Morphology
T.9.3. Syntax
T.9.4. Lexis
T.9.5. Language activities
T.9.6. Language functions
T.9.7. Language situations
T.9.8. Referential objects

T.10 Skills developed by the course

T.10.1. Understanding of speech
T.10.2. Understanding of written material

T.10.3. Speaking
T.10.4. Writing

T.11. Course level

T.11.1. Beginners
T.11.2. False beginners
T.11.4. Intermediate
T.11.4. Advanced
T.11.5. Further training

T.12. Material used in course

T.12.1. Ideas regarding desired material
T.12.2. Reference to known material

T.13. Course methods

T.13.1. Ideas regarding method desired
T.13.2. Reference to known method

Possible steps to be taken by the learner

S.1. Consulting prospectuses of teaching establishments
S.2. Consulting syllabuses of teaching establishments
S.3. Consulting one or more teaching establishment
S.4. Consulting an advisory service
S.5. Consulting someone with experience of a type of course

Means of obtaining information

M.1. Questionnaires
M.2. Attitude scales
M.3. Interviews

IV.D During the course

The learners' resources may perhaps have altered during the course; or again his objectives may have changed or he may want or have to obtain a different kind of certificate from the one originally chosen. All such possible alterations will have their repercussions on the curriculum taken and the learner must know how he can continue his studies, what are the possibilities offered by the teaching establishment and what fresh compromises he can find there.

Types of information

T.1. Types of establishment

T.1.1. Is it necessary for the learner to move to another establishment for any reason?

T.2. Time needed by the syllabus

T.2.1. Is the timetable chosen still adequate?

T.3. Place where learning is done

T.3.1. Does the learner need to change to another place for any reason?

T.4. Cost of course

T.4.1. Do any changes in financial resources involve an alteration of the syllabus chosen?

T.5. Teacher

T.5.1. Should there be a change of teacher for any reason?

T.6. Learners

T.6.1. Should the learner change to another group?

T.7. Technical aids to learning

T.7.1. Do other objectives call for the use of different technical aids?

T.8. Areas in which curriculum is used

T.8.1. Are the original areas of use still valid?

T.9. Content of syllabus

T.9.1. Do other objectives or methods of assessment call for changes in content?

T.10. Skills developed by the syllabus

T.10.1. Should one skill be developed more or less than another?

T.11. Course level

T.11.1. Is a change of level necessary?

T.12. Material used in course

T.12.1. Is the material used suitable?

T.13. Course methods

T.13.1. Do the method(s) used come up to the learner's expectations?

Possible steps to be taken by the learner

S.1. Negotiating alterations with the establishment
S.2. Changing to another establishment

Means of obtaining information

M.1. Interviews
M.2. Questionnaires
M.3. Observations

6. IDENTIFICATION OF THE LEARNER'S NEEDS BY THE TEACHING ESTABLISHMENT

V. Identification of the learner's needs by the teaching establishment in relation to its resources

V.B Before the course

It is extremely advisable for a teaching establishment to improve its knowledge of the needs of future learners. This is a means of developing its policy in line with demand. It is therefore important that the establishment also take stock of its resources so as to find out what possibilities it has of making adjustments and taking the needs of its students into consideration. Acting indirectly in relation to them and directly in collaboration with them it will define its own objectives and the methods of assessing them and suggest suitable curricula. The wider the range it can offer, the more chance it will have of meeting the needs of the greatest number; but the more resources it must have to draw on.

Types of information

T.1. Types of establishment

T.1.1. Private establishments providing only language courses for adults
T.1.2. Private establishments teaching languages among other subjects
T.1.3. Official or semi-official establishments providing only language courses for adults
T.1.4. Official or semi-official establishments teaching other subjects besides languages
T.1.5. Private or public vocational schools offering language courses
T.1.6. Centres, institutes and research and teaching departments attached to a university and giving language tuition
T.1.7. Training centres attached to a firm or other establishment where languages are used
T.1.8. Radio and television services broadcasting language courses
T.1.9. Firms selling language correspondence courses
T.1.10. Firms selling self-tuition courses

T.2. Reputation

T.2.1. What is the establishment's own idea of itself?
T.2.2. How is it regarded by outsiders?

T.3. Staff

T.3.1. Number of people employed on administrative duties
T.3.2. Secretariat
T.3.3. Educational executives
T.3.4. Educational advisers ⎱
T.3.5. Research staff   ⎰ What are their native languages?
T.3.6. Staff engaged on planning courses

T.3.7. Staff engaged on producing courses } What are their native
T.3.8. Staff engaged on implementing courses } languages?
T.3.9. Teachers

T.4. Length of time employed

T.4.1. People employed full-time
T.4.2. People employed part-time
T.4.3. People engaged for one specific job
T.4.4. Number of hours per teacher
T.4.5. Distribution of courses in time
T.4.5.1. Extended courses (several hours a week)
T.4.5.2. Intensive courses (several hours a day)
T.4.5.3. Courses extending over the full year
T.4.5.4. Courses confined to a particular time of the year
T.4.5.5. 'A la carte' courses
T.4.5.6. Courses starting at frequent intervals
T.4.5.7. Courses starting at longer intervals
T.4.6. Time devoted to research
T.4.7. Time devoted to planning
T.4.8. Time devoted to implementing courses
T.4.9. Time devoted to producing courses
T.4.10 Time devoted to guidance work

T.5. Places and methods of setting up establishments

T.5.1. Number of establishments set up
T.5.2. Country
T.5.3. Region
T.5.4. Small places
T.5.5. Average-sized town
T.5.6. Large town
T.5.7. Correspondence or broadcast courses
T.5.8. Type of building
T.5.9. Number of rooms for administration
T.5.10. Number of rooms for teaching
T.5.11. Number of rooms for research
T.5.12. Number of rooms for guidance work
T.5.13. Types of rooms

T.6. Number of languages taught

T.7. Financial arrangements

T.7.1. Profit-making establishment
T.7.2. Non-profit-making establishment
T.7.3. Cost of courses
T.7.4. Salaries paid to various types of employees
T.7.5. Operational budget
T.7.6. Research budget
T.7.7. Guidance work budget
T.7.8. Planning budget

T.7.9.   Budget devoted to implementing courses
T.7.10.   Budget devoted to production of courses

Possible steps to be taken by the teaching establishment

S.1.   As a general rule teaching establishments do keep this kind of information up to date
S.2.   In order to obtain fuller information they may also consult an organization specializing in institutional analysis.

Means of obtaining information

M.1.   Statistics
M.2.   Questionnaires

V.D During the course

As we have seen, the learner's needs may change during the course. If a teaching establishment wishes to apply a systems approach centred on individuals or groups learning a language there, it must normally be capable of making allowance for these changes and thus altering its resources to suit the new needs. Here we come up against the whole problem of the adaptability and flexibility of institutional structures to which there is usually no solution. However, it is on this factor that success or failure of the possible applications of the systems approach outlined in this study depends.

In order that they may be able to make the necessary decisions enabling them to arrive at new compromises with the learners, teaching establishments must regularly ask themselves a number of questions concerning changes to be made as regards time, place, staff and financial resources.

Types of information

T.1.   Types of establishment

T.1.1.   Should any change be made in the status of the establishment?

T.2.   Reputation

T.2.1.   Is it necessary to bring about any change in the establishment's reputation?
T.2.2.   Is its reputation altering of its own accord?

T.3.   Staff

T.3.1.   Is there any need for changes in the number, jobs and duties of the various classes of people employed at the establishment?

T.4.   Length of time employed

T.4.1.   Is there any need for changes in the time spent on teaching and the time devoted by staff to the establishment's various activities?

T.5.   Place and method of setting up establishment

T.5.1.   Would it be advisable to open other teaching centres or to close down some?

T.6. Financial arrangements

T.6.1. What effect do decisions made have on financial resources, salaries, budgets and the cost of courses?

Possible steps to be taken by the teaching establishment

S.1. Decisions taken after analysis of demand from a given section of the population
S.2. Negotiation with learners
S.3. Fresh advertising
S.4. Introduction of flexible, adaptable structures
S.5. Increasing capabilities of adaptation

Means of obtaining information

M.1. Surveys
M.2. Sample surveys
M.3. Questionnaires

VI. Identification of the learner's needs by the teaching establishment in relation to its objectives

VI.B Before the course

Like learners, teaching establishments very often have only a vague idea of the objectives they seek to attain through the instruction given. If they wish to adopt unit/credit systems they will need to define them precisely at two levels – general and operational so that in the first place they may offer them to future learners and discuss them with them and secondly so that they may be in a position to help the learners to fix their own objectives. Like them they must make the same effort to become aware by whom and in what manner the aims of their teaching are defined and what pressures and influences the establishments can directly or indirectly bring to bear on the learner.

Types of information

T.1. Level of description of objectives

T.1.1. Long-term objectives
T.1.1.1. General objectives
T.1.1.2. Operational objectives
T.1.2. Short-term objectives
T.1.2.1. General objectives
T.1.2.2. Operational objectives

T.2. Areas in which the language is intended to be used

T.2.1. Private life
T.2.2. Working life

T.3.1.   Phonetics
T.3.2.   Morphology
T.3.3.   Syntax
T.3.4.   Lexis
T.3.5.   Referential objects
T.3.6.   Language activities
T.3.7.   Language functions
T.3.8.   Language situations
T.3.9.   Understanding speech
T.3.10.   Understanding written matter
T.3.11.   Speaking
T.3.12.   Writing
T.3.13.   General content (textbooks, methods, threshold level)

T.4. Who defines the objectives?

T.4.1.   The administrative section
T.4.2.   The educational section
T.4.3.   The teachers
T.4.4.   The learners
T.4.5.   The material used
T.4.6.   Through negotiation

T.5. Who supplies information about the objectives?

T.5.1.   Publicity materials
T.5.2.   The Secretariat
T.5.3.   The educational section
T.5.4.   The teacher

T.6. In what form?

T.6.1.   In prospectuses, advertisements, by demonstrations
T.6.2.   In syllabuses
T.6.3.   In pre-prepared lists (eg threshold levels)
T.6.4.   In the material used
T.6.5.   In the teaching
T.6.6.   In interviews

Possible steps to be taken by the teaching establishment

S.1.   Acceptance of objectives laid down in the material used
S.2.   Altering those objectives and producing suitable additional material
S.3.   Defining objectives and selecting appropriate material
S.4.   Discussing the objectives with learners and defining them jointly with the latter
S.5.   Discussing pre-prepared lists of objectives with the learners

Means of obtaining information

M.1.   Interviews

M.2.   Pre-prepared lists of objectives
M.3.   Methods of defining objectives

VI.D During the course

In learner-centred systems, specification of objectives must not take place only before the course but must continue throughout. The role of the teacher becomes vital here since it is up to him to introduce permanent procedures for defining, discussing and revising and to make sure that they are used. His task will be made easier if such procedures are an integral part of the material, failing which he will be obliged to adopt a personal method of teaching by objectives. The establishment, for its part, must have fairly adaptable organisational structures so that it may amend its own objectives in line with those of the learners.

The types of information to be collected are the same as those specified earlier under VI.B, so that we need only repeat the chapter headings.

Types of information

T.1.   Level of description of objectives

T.2.   Areas in which the language is intended to be used

T.3.   Content of objectives

T.4.   Who defines the objectives?

T.5.   Who supplies information on the objectives?

T.6.   In what form?

Possible steps to be taken by the teaching establishment

S.1.   Making definition, discussion and revision procedures an integral part of the material
S.2.   Training the teachers in the practice of teaching by objectives
S.3.   Creating adaptable institutional structures

Means of obtaining information

M.1.   Interviews
M.2.   Methods of defining objectives
M.3.   Pre-prepared lists of objectives
M.4.   Questionnaires forming an integral part of the material

VII. Identification of the learner's needs by the teaching establishment in relation to its methods of assessment

VII.B Before the course

The study *Survey of curricula and performance in modern languages 1971–72* by C V James and S Rouve clearly showed how the methods of assessment used by some establishments failed to match up either to their curricula or to their definition of learning needs, where any such existed. It cannot be too often repeated that specification and assessment go hand in hand, that they cannot be separated one from another and that teaching establishments must have the necessary means of making them an integral part of the actual teaching systems they introduced.

Before the course it will be necessary to collect information enabling the teaching establishment to be organized in line with what has been achieved, the interests and personalities of the learners and the types of certificate awarded by the establishment.

Types of information

T.1.   Assessment of what has been achieved

T.1.1.   Phonetics
T.1.2.   Morphology
T.1.3.   Syntax
T.1.4.   Lexis
T.1.5.   Referential objects
T.1.6.   Language activities
T.1.7.   Language functions
T.1.8.   Language situations
T.1.9.   Understanding speech
T.1.10.   Reading
T.1.11.   Speaking
T.1.12.   Writing
T.1.13.   General content (textbooks, methods, threshold levels)

T.2.   Type of assessment

T.2.1.   Objective tests
T.2.2.   Interviews
T.2.3.   Reference to background, *cf* III.B, T.1.
T.2.4.   Questionnaires
T.2.5.   Entrance examinations
T.2.6.   Entrance competitions

T.3.   Assessment of the learner's identity and personality

T.3.1.   *cf* I.B, T.1. and T.2.

T.4.   Assessment of interests

T.4.1.   Areas in working life
T.4.2.   Areas in private life

T.5.   Grouping of learners

T.5.1.   By reference to what they have achieved
T.5.2.   By reference to interests
T.5.3.   By reference to personality
T.5.4.   By reference to identity (age, occupation)
T.5.5.   By reference to language background
T.5.6.   By reference to methods chosen (language laboratory, audio-visual methods etc)

T.5.7. By reference to resources (time, place, financial resources etc)
T.5.8. By reference to objectives
T.5.9. By reference to course chosen (size of group, profile of teacher etc)

T.6. Types of qualification

T.6.1. Official diploma
T.6.2. Non-official diploma
T.6.3. Testimonial
T.6.4. Certificate
T.6.5. Unit/credit
T.6.6. With marks
T.6.7. Without marks
T.6.8. With comments
T.6.9. Without comments

T.7. Content of qualification

T.7.1. *cf* T.1. above

Possible steps to be taken by teaching establishment

S.1. Provide the necessary means of assessment
S.2. Organize a guidance service

Means of obtaining information

M.1. Aptitude tests
M.2. Personality tests
M.3. Attitude scales
M.4. Tests of aptitude for languages
M.5. Selection tests
M.6. Classification tests
M.7. Questionnaires
M.8. Interviews

VII.D During the course

Assessment during the course is intended firstly to enable the learner to find his feet *vis-à-vis* the instruction he is to take and secondly to enable the establishment to have a permanent check on whether the teaching systems used are suitable and whether they are functioning properly. In this connection we use the types of information specified under III.D, together with those enabling an assessment to be made of the operation of the systems as a whole.

Types of information

T.1. Conditions of assessment
   cf III.D, T.1.

T.2. Types of assessment
   cf III.D, T.2.

T.7. Technical aids to learning

T.7.1.   Language laboratory
T.7.2.   Television
T.7.3.   Radio
T.7.4.   Teaching machines
T.7.5.   Film stills
T.7.6.   Slides
T.7.7.   Films
T.7.8.   Other visual aids
T.7.9.   Recorded tapes
T.7.10   Cassettes
T.7.11. Records
T.7.12. Other auditive aids
T.7.13. Printed matter

T.8. Material used in the course

T.8.1.   Material bought on the market
T.8.2.   Original material
T.8.3.   Additional original material
T.8.4.   One-off material
T.8.5.   Material in several copies

T.9. Areas in which curriculum is used

T.9.1.   Working life
T.9.2.   Private life

T.10. Content of course
     cf VI.B, T.3.

T.11. Methods used in the course

T.11.1. Method determined by the material
T.11.2. Original methods
T.11.3. Additional original activities
T.11.4   Method depending on the teacher

T.12. Levels taught

T.12.1. Beginners
T.12.2. False beginners
T.12.3. Intermediate stage
T.12.4. Advanced stage
T.12.5. Further training stage

Possible steps to be taken by the teaching establishment

S.1.   Describing curricula in detail but so as to be understandable to a non-specialist
S.2.   Negotiating curricula with the learner in order to arrive at a compromise between his needs and the establishment's facilities for meeting them

Means of obtaining information

M.1.   Questionnaires
M.2.   Interviews

VIII.D During the course

Since the learner's needs will change during the course, the teaching establishment should be capable of adapting its syllabuses in line with changes as they are confirmed. Obviously this requires flexible organizational structures such as are in most cases incompatible with institutional rigidity. The attempt to achieve such flexibility is, however, one of the main conditions for the use of unit/credit systems of learning. Thus the teaching establishment must constantly raise certain questions regarding the different component parts of its syllabuses so that where necessary it may decide to alter some of them.

Types of information

T.1.   Types of establishment

T.1.1.   Will changes made in the syllabuses make any difference to the establishment's status and reputation?

T.2.   Time taken up by the syllabus

T.2.1.   Is it necessary to change the amount of time devoted to syllabuses?

T.3.   Where teaching is done

T.3.1.   Is it necessary to make any changes in the places where the courses are held?

T.4.   Cost of course

T.4.1.   Should the cost of courses be increased or reduced?

T.5.   Teachers

T.5.1.   Would it be advisable to make any change in the length of time teachers are employed?
T.5.2.   Do they need retraining?
T.5.3.   Do any teachers need to be recruited or dismissed?

T.6.   Learners

T.6.1.   Must the composition of groups necessarily be altered?

T.7.   Technical aids to learning

T.7.1.   Should any technical aids be purchased or disposed of?
T.7.2.   Should other uses of them be contemplated?

T.8.   Material used in the course

T.8.1.   Should further material be purchased or produced?

T.9.   Areas in which curriculum is used

T.9.1.   Is there need to specialize in any sphere?
T.9.2.   Should any areas be added or dropped?

T.10. Contents of syllabus

T.10.1. Is there a need for changes in the contents of the syllabus?

T.11. Methods used in the course

T.11.1. Is it necessary to make any change in the methods used?

T.12. Grades taught

T.12.1. Is it necessary to distinguish differently between the levels of syllabuses?
T.12.2. Is it necessary to add or drop courses at certain levels?

Possible steps to be taken by the teaching establishment

S.1. Negotiate possible desirable changes with the learners
S.2. Introduce flexible organizational structures
S.3. Increase capabilities of adjustment

Means of obtaining information

M.1. Interviews
M.2. Questionnaires
M.3. Observation
M.4. Content analysis

7. IDENTIFICATION OF THE LEARNER'S NEEDS BY THE USER-INSTITUTION

IX. Identification of the learner's needs by the user-institution in relation to its resources

By user-institution we mean any structurized social unit making use of one or more foreign languages to enable it to operate properly. This therefore includes both large firms or businesses and administrative bodies and small traders or families. In any given society it is they who are more or less responsible for directly or indirectly determining the needs of learners and teaching establishments. It may be found that information circulates somewhat inefficiently between the different levels and that the expression of an individual's needs is subject to all kinds of pressures and censoring from teaching bodies, users and society.

The identification of needs carried out in or by these institutions is extremely important because it is here that we can observe the real use of foreign languages, thus enabling us to secure information from which to specify objectives and syllabuses. We are here looking mainly at those user-institutions which undertake to provide language tuition for their employees either by giving them opportunities of learning at the institution's own centres or by sending them to an outside establishment. We shall make use of the same outline as previously but without the heading 'During the course' since they are not themselves directly involved in teaching; and we shall restrict the types of information because to describe these in detail would take up too much space in this study.

Types of information

T.1. Types of institution

T.1.1.   National and local government services
T.1.2.   Private businesses

T.2. Staff

T.2.1.   Number employed
T.2.2.   In administration
T.2.3.   In technical work
T.2.4.   In manufacture
T.2.5.   In training duties
T.2.6.   In personnel section
T.2.7.   Management
T.2.8.   Executives
T.2.9.   Clerical workers
T.2.10.   Manual workers
T.2.11.   Labourers

T.3. Length of time employed

T.3.1.   Full-time staff
T.3.2.   Part-time staff

T.3.3. People employed for a particular job
T.3.4. Hours of work
T.3.5. Time devoted to training
T.3.6. Study leave

T.4. Place and location

T.4.1. Number of establishments
T.4.2. Type of building
T.4.3. Type of premises
T.4.4. Country
T.4.5. Region
T.4.6. Small place
T.4.7. Average-sized town
T.4.8. Large town
T.4.9. City suburbs
T.4.10. City centre

T.5. Financial arrangements

T.5.1. General budget
T.5.2. Budgets for different sections
T.5.3. Wages and salaries of various classes of employee

Possible steps to be taken by the user-institution

S.1. User-institutions usually keep this kind of information up to date
S.2. In order to obtain fuller information they may also consult an organization specializing in institutional analysis

Means of obtaining information

M.1. Statistics
M.2. Questionnaires

X. Identification of the learner's needs by the user-institution in relation to its objectives

At user-institution level the identification of needs in relation to objectives will consist mainly in describing what the people living and working there do with the language or languages used.

From this description they can proceed to define the objectives and curricula best suited to requirements

Types of information

T.1. Level of description of objectives

T.1.1. General objectives
T.1.2. Operational objectives

T.2.   Areas in which used

T.2.1.   At work
T.2.2.   In private life

T.3.   Content of objectives

T.3.1.   Language activities
T.3.2.   Language functions
T.3.3.   Language situations
T.3.4.   Referential objects

T.4.   Language skills practised

T.4.1.   Understanding speech
T.4.2.   Understanding writing
T.4.3.   Speaking
T.4.4.   Writing

T.5.   Frequency with which languages are used

T.5.1.   Frequently
T.5.2.   Occasionally
T.5.3.   Rarely

T.6.   Who defines the objectives

T.6.1.   The user
T.6.2.   The personnel department
T.6.3.   An internal teaching establishment
T.6.4.   An external teaching establishment
T.6.5.   A body specializing in institutional analysis
T.6.6.   An internal observer
T.6.7.   An external observer
T.6.8.   By negotiation (trade unions, employers' associations, works councils)

Possible steps to be taken by the user-institution

S.1.   Making an analysis of its own means
S.2.   Consulting a body specializing in institutional analysis
S.3.   Consulting a teaching establishment

Means of obtaining information

M.1.   Questionnaires
M.2.   Interviews
M.3.   Observation
M.4.   Job analysis
M.5.   Content analysis

XI. Identification of the learner's needs by the user-institution in relation to its methods of assessment

It is essential that the individual should know how his abilities are going to be assessed by the user-institution and that the latter should clearly understand – which is not always the case – the criteria adopted by it for such assessment, the results of which may have a decisive influence on the behaviour, motivations and attitudes of the users. The latter should be able to share in their own assessment.

Types of information

T.1. Assessment on enrolment

T.1.1. Tests of aptitude for the language or languages
T.1.2. Selection tests
T.1.3. Classification tests
T.1.4. Personality tests
T.1.5. Psychological aptitude tests
T.1.6. Interviews
T.1.7. Competitive tests
T.1.8. Examinations

T.2. Types of qualification demanded

T.2.1. University degree
T.2.2. Professional or vocational qualification
T.2.3. School-leaving certificate giving access to a university
T.2.4. Diploma, testimonial or certificate issued by a private school
T.2.5. Diploma, testimonial or certificate issued by an official or semi-official permanent education establishment
T.2.6. References
T.2.7. Recommendations
T.2.8. Certificate issued by another user-institution

T.3. Continuous assessment

T.3.1. Observation and supervision at place where language is used
T.3.2. Periodical interviews
T.3.3. Periodical examinations
T.3.4. Competitive tests leading to promotion
T.3.5. Objective tests given periodically

T.4. Result of assessment

T.4.1. Promotion to a higher job
T.4.2. Social promotion
T.4.3. Increase in salary
T.4.4. Increased responsibility
T.4.5. Wider choice of jobs
T.4.6. More varied tasks
T.4.7. Opportunity for training
T.4.8. Dismissal

T.5.1.   A colleague
T.5.2.   A superior
T.5.3.   The personnel department
T.5.4.   The management
T.5.5.   An outsider observer
T.5.6.   The user himself
T.5.7.   A teaching establishment
T.5.8.   A group of colleagues
T.5.9.   A mixed group (eg 5.1. + 5.2. + 5.5.)

Possible steps to be taken by the user-institutions

S.1.   Laying down coherent criteria for engaging, assessing and promoting
S.2.   Arranging for the user to have a share in his own assessment

Means of obtaining information

M.1.   Observation
M.2.   Interviews
M.3.   Different kinds of psychological tests
M.4.   Different kinds of language tests

XII. Identification of the learner's needs by the user-institution in relation to its programmes

In the case of user-institutions the term 'programme' must be understood to mean the methods, opportunities and facilities which they offer to individuals for learning one or more foreign languages. The institutions themselves will not give training as such, except by the use which they make of the language or languages in their work, and they will have to turn to either an internal teaching centre or an outside establishment in order to negotiate jointly with them and the future learner the syllabuses as these have been described under VIII.B.

Types of information

T.1.   Time spent on training

T.1.1.   Courses taken partly during working time
T.1.2.   Courses taken entirely during working time (continuous or non-continuous study leave)
T.1.3.   Courses taken entirely outside working hours
T.1.4.   Length of course

T.2.   Place where courses are taken

T.2.1.   At an internal teaching centre
T.2.2.   At an external teaching establishment
T.2.3.   At the place of work
T.2.4.   At home

T.3. Payment for training

T.3.1. Paid by the institution
T.3.2. Paid by the public authorities
T.3.3. Full payment provided
T.3.4. Part payment provided
T.3.5. Study leave on full pay
T.3.6. Study leave on part pay
T.3.7. Unpaid study leave

T.4. Learners

T.4.1. Number of persons whose courses are partially paid for
T.4.2. Number of persons whose courses are fully paid for

T.5. Syllabuses

   cf. VIII.B, 1 to 12

Possible steps to be taken by the user-institution

S.1. Inform individuals of their entitlement to training and the facilities available
S.2. User-institution's training programmes
S.3. Negotiate courses with the centre or the teaching establishment
S.4. Negotiate training programmes with the future learners

Means of obtaining information

M.1. Interviews
M.2. Questionnaires

APPENDIX I: IDENTIFYING LANGUAGE NEEDS IN FOUR DIFFERENT CASES

Types of information to be obtained for Case 1:

A person who wants to learn English, enrolls at a teaching establishment and studies there

(The numbers and letters refer to those in the section 'Types of information')

Before the course		During the course	
Essential	**Advisable**	**Essential**	**Advisable**
I B T1, T3, T4, T5	T2	I D T3, T4, T5	T1, T2
II B T1, T3	T2, T4	II D T3, T4	T1, T2
III B T1, T2, T3	T4	III D T2, T4	T1, T3
IV B T1, T2, T3, T4, T9, T11	T5, T6, T7, T8 T10, T12, T13	IV D T1, T2, T3, T4, T9, T11	T5, T6, T7, T8, T10, T12, T13

Types of information to be obtained for Case 2:

A person who wants to learn German and is learning it by self-tuition merely for pleasure

Before the course		During the course	
Essential	**Advisable**	**Essential**	**Advisable**
I B T1, T5	T2, T3	I D T2, T3, T5	T1, T4
II B T3	T1, T2, T4	II D T4	T1, T2, T3
III B T1	T2, T3, T4	III D	T1, T2, T3, T4
IV B T4	T2, T7, T9, T10, T11, T12, T13	IV D T4	T2, T7, T8, T9, T10, T11, T12

Types of information to be obtained for Case 3:

A teaching establishment that wants to organize and adapt its methods of teaching French to fit in with the demand

Before the course		During the course	
Essential	**Advisable**	**Essential**	**Advisable**
I B T1, T3, T4, T5	T2	I D T2, T3, T4, T5	T1
II B T1, T3, T4	T2	II D T1, T3	T2, T4
III B T1, T2, T3	T4	III D T2, T3, T4	T1
IV B T2, T3, T4, T6 T9, T10, T11	T5, T7, T8, T12, T13	IV D T2, T3, T4, T5, T6, T7, T8, T9, T10, T11, T12, T13	T1
V B T1, T4, T7	T2, T3, T5, T6	V D T3, T4, T5, T6	T1, T2
VI B T1, T3	T2, T4, T5, T6	VI D T1, T3	T2, T4, T5, T6
VII B T1, T2, T5, T6, T7	T3, T4	VII D T1, T2, T3, T4, T5, T6, T7, T8	
VIII B T1, T2, T4, T5 T6, T7, T8, T10, T11, T12	T3, T9	VIII D T1, T2, T3, T4 T5, T6, T7, T8, T9, T10, T11, T12	
IX B			
X T3	T1, T2, T4, T5, T6		
XI T1, T2	T3, T4, T5		
XII	T1, T3, T5		

Types of information to be obtained for Case 4:

A user-institution that has decided to give its commercial executives a knowledge of Spanish to enable them to canvass South-American markets

		Essential			Advisable
I	B	T1, T3, T4, T5	I	B	T2
II	B		II	B	T1, T2, T3, T4
III	B	T1, T2, T3, T4			
IV	B	T1, T2, T3, T4, T11	IV	B	T5, T6, T7, T8, T9, T10, T12, T13
V	B		V	B	T1, T2, T4, T5, T7
VI	B		VI	B	T1, T2, T3, T4, T5, T6
VII	B	T6	VII	B	T1, T2, T4, T5, T7
VIII	B		VIII	B	T1, T2, T3, T4, T5, T6, T7, T8, T9, T10, T11, T12
IX		T1, T2, T3, T4, T5			
X		T1, T2, T3, T4, T5, T6			
XI		T1, T2, T3, T4, T5			
XII		T1, T2, T3, T4, T5			

Extract II.3

J A van Ek, *Foreign language learning needs in schools* (original paper)

It is becoming commonplace to say that teaching and learning must be needs-orientated, that the objectives of a learning programme must specify the abilities that are needed by the learners.

With regard to foreign-language learning, this may mean that the objective specifies the ability to read scientific texts in Russian, or, to give another example, to explain the menu to English-speaking guests in a restaurant, to take their orders and to settle the bill with them. Needs analysis of adult target groups or of learners in vocational training may lead to the formulation of such objectives. The problem in general education is, of course, that we do not know what our pupils may need the foreign language for; we don't even know whether they will ever be called upon to use a foreign language at all or, if so, which language. Stating this problem is nothing else than stating the problem of determining the content of general education. What to teach to pupils whose future life is still shrouded in the mists of time? The usual answer – and I don't see there could be a better answer – is that one tries to prepare them as well as possible for their future life whatever this may be, that one tries to equip them as well as possible for fulfilling their potential as individuals in a highly complex and constantly changing society.

In this perspective the ability to communicate in at least one foreign language, preferably a language of wide international currency, would seem to be a valid and worthwhile learning goal. The justification is very simply that one's options for choosing one's way of life in our modern society are unacceptably limited if one does not possess this ability. As Louis Porcher formulates it in his excellent study for the Council of Europe called *Interrogations sur les besoins langagiers en contextes scolaires*, to which the present paper owes a good deal: 'On peut considérer en tout cas que maîtriser correctement une langue comme outil de communication, correspond désormais à un besoin moyen pour tout homme.

This, then, is our first, and, for us as language teachers, central point of orientation: the ability to communicate in a foreign language. It does not yet supply us with a concrete objective, not to mention the content of a learning programme. Yet we know it is not the same thing as knowledge of the grammar of the foreign language, mastery of the 2,000 most frequent vocabulary items and/or the ability to translate sentences from the native language into the foreign language and vice versa. If communicative ability is our aim, we must describe, analyse and specify this ability in its own terms, in its own categories. It is only after this that we may determine what grammatical apparatus, what vocabulary, etc. are most suitable to achieve this ability. Our learners being general learners, we shall primarily wish to provide them with the ability to communicate in general circumstances about general subjects, or rather subjects of general importance and interest. There is a wide variety of such subjects and we cannot take them all even in a course of several years' duration. We are therefore, as usual in defining objectives and devising learning-programmes, obliged to make a choice. And then, obviously, we will choose those subjects that are most likely to be of interest to the learners, either in their present situation – as learners of a certain age in a certain sociocultural and educational situation – or with a view to

67

likely future situations. It would seem equally obvious that the learners' active participation is sought in the choice of these subjects – or *topics* as we usually call them. The more interested and involved the learners are, the more likely they are to make the effort required in order to actually learn something. But will this really prepare the pupils for their future life? Will this not fix them at a stage of development which should be transitory, and, above all, will their participation in the choice not lead to chaos? Fortunately, the nature of communication and of language is such that we need not be unduly worried about this. However varied concrete manifestations may be, communication and language each have a hard common core, a core that forms the backbone of language use whatever the topic may be. With respect to communication, this core is constituted by the general communicative functions such as stating, asking, denying, correcting, expressing doubt, expressing ability, willingness or unwillingness, etc. etc., together with such general notions as presence/absence, before and after, past/present/future, causality, contrast, etc. Whenever we communicate we fulfil such language-functions and we handle such general notions. Similarly with regard to the actual language forms that we use: inevitably these reflect the formal structure of the language, its structural properties. All this means, of course, that whatever topic of communication we choose and practise, the learners will inevitably be exposed to the common core both of comunication and of language. In other words, in the perspective of the acquisition of general communicative ability the actual choice of topics is of secondary importance as long as this common core, which is the basis of transfer-potential, is adequately present. Even so, there is remarkable agreement on what topics are of really general interest and are therefore to be given a high-priority index. Most teachers, and, given the choice, most pupils rank such topics as 'identification of self and others', 'family and friends', 'interests and pastimes', 'food and accommodation', etc., high on their list of priorities. This means that most people seem to be interested in – or rather seem to feel the need for – being able to say who and what they are and to find out who and what others are, to describe their family and friends, to talk about what they like doing in their spare time, about such things as where they live or would like to live, etc. In planning a learning programme, those responsible for it will take these interests into account and see to it that, in practising communication about these topics, the essential language functions and general notions as well as the most fundamental formal characteristics of the language are duly represented. When what is now known as the 'functional-notional approach' was first presented, concern, doubt and even disbelief was often expressed about the possibility of integrating a sound structural progression into a learning programme based on a communicative syllabus. By now such scepsis can only reflect ignorance of what has actually been done in this field. There are now several language courses, notably for English, that demonstrate the feasibility of integrating structural progression into a functional-notional framework. The key is the principle of recycling. The most important functions are first practised with structurally very simple language material and are reintroduced at later stages in the course with successively more complex language forms.

A framework for the description, analysis and specification of communicative ability was developed in the Modern Languages Project of the Council of Europe and first presented and applied in my study called *The Threshold Level in a European unit/credit system for modern language learning by adults* (Strasbourg 1975), followed by *The threshold level for modern language learning in schools*, published by Longman in 1977. The *Threshold Level* contains detailed specifications both of the common core and of topics which, by common agreement, may be regarded as of general interest to adult learners and to learners in schools respectively. The *Threshold Level* (for English) has meanwhile been followed by similar specifications for Spanish, German, Italian and Danish and by *Un niveau-seuil* for French, including a version for schools.

So far we have taken as our point of orientation the need of the learners to acquire communicative ability in a foreign language and we have seen what this communicative ability may involve. More exactly, our first point of orientation has been the communicative ability itself. Our second point of orientation will be more strictly the learner himself or herself. 'In an educational context', John Trim points out, 'we are not simply concerned with training certain kinds of skilled behaviour, but also [. . .] with the steady and purposive development of the learner as a communicator and as a learner as well as his personal and social development'. The quotation is from Trim's report[1] on the work of a working party set up in 1979 by the Modern Languages Project Group to consider 'an overall model for the specification of language learning objectives more complex than those set out in the Threshold Level documents'.

To start with the learner as a communicator: 'We are obliged', to quote John Trim again, 'to see communication as a process by which two (or more) individuals, each with a different experiential background, use speech on the basis of a partly shared, but always distinct, language model, to come to terms with each other and the requirements of a social situation involving them both. If we are to educate young people, or adults, to participate effectively in social co-operation and what J R Firth once called "speech fellowship", we are as much concerned with the formation of attitudes and personality development as we are with the inculcation of knowledge and skills.'

'It is of course much more difficult', Trim goes on to say, 'if not impossible, to convert an aim of this kind into explicit behavioural objectives. Nevertheless, we need to monitor carefully the teaching methods and tests we employ in order to ensure that, in pursuing the operational objectives we can make explicit, we do not find that we are in fact blocking the proper development of the type of communicative personality we ought to be promoting.' To reformulate the last part of this quotation: Be sure not to teach only that which can be tested objectively!

Let us now consider the development of the learner as a learner. The end of the compulsory school period is not, cannot be, the end of learning. In order to meet the rapidly changing demands of life in our modern society, in order to cope with increasingly rapid developments affecting the position of the individual in this society, learning must be a lifelong process. With regard to pupils in compulsory education, we do not know what occupations or professions they will engage in in later life and we do not even know what society will be like when they have grown up. This means that, in order to equip them for their future life, it is of paramount importance not only to provide them with knowledge and skills that are relevant *now* but to prepare them for the acquisition of such knowledge and skills as they may need later on in life. This is to say that the pupils should be prepared for further learning. School is the great organized educational experience in everyone's life. School may whet the

[1] Included in the present volume as Extract III.3.

appetite for further learning; it may also spoil it for ever. With regard to our theme, needs, I would even go as far as to say that one of the strongest needs of our pupils in order to cope in their future lives is exactly this: to have their appetite whetted for further learning. What does this involve? First and foremost, the experience of successful learning. No pupil whose educational record is a persistent record of failures can be expected to voluntarily undertake any further learning tasks after leaving school. On the other hand, pupils who experience success in learning, who have gained confidence in their ability to learn what they want or need to learn will not so quickly shy away from further learning tasks. They will be confident that, if only they make the required effort, they can achieve something. However, if this confidence is based on not more than good marks, an occasional pat on the back by the teacher, and a school-leaving diploma, it is not all that certain that making an effort will guarantee success in further learning. We all know people who failed miserably in higher education, in spite of an above-average school record. What is needed is not only that the learners possess confidence in their own abilities but that they have also acquired learning-skills, that they know how to learn. As foreign-language teachers we can contribute both to the gaining of confidence and to the acquisition of learning skills. The communicative approach, if used properly, is particularly suitable for making learners experience learning success and thus giving them confidence in their abilities. This was different in the traditional grammar-translation method, where success required highly-developed powers of abstraction and reflection. If the aim of our teaching is not primarily grammatical finesse but communicative ability, every single pupil can experience some degree of success. Of course, some are more intelligent than others and some are linguistically more gifted than others, but given appropriate learning opportunities no pupil will totally fail to acquire any communicative ability at all. This is because communication can be achieved at many different levels of sophistication and subtlety and with many different degrees of formal correctness. Surely, every pupil can learn to use 'perhaps' in order to express doubt but not everyone will easily or perhaps at all learn to use sentences such as 'presumably it might be true'. Communicative acts can often be performed with a wide variety of linguistic means, ranging from structurally extremely simple ones to bafflingly complex ones. The realization that simple means will often suffice to communicate effectively is a big step towards acquiring confidence, and, given proper guidance, every mentally normal pupil can make this step. Confidence is necessary for further learning but, as we saw, it is not a sufficient condition; it does not guarantee success in further learning unless the pupil knows how to learn. The inculcation of learning skills is a more complex task than providing learners with some confidence. Of course it is not that difficult to teach pupils how to use a dictionary or even how to cope with unknown elements in a text if no dictionary is available. What makes it complex is that learning processes are so greatly varied and individual, that what is the best procedure for one person may not be the best for another. Another factor of its complexity is that after leaving school learners may have to carry out learning tasks under very different conditions than when they were at school. They will rarely have the intensive guidance and monitoring that the school system provides; they will usually be much more if not entirely on their own. This means that the school should prepare learners to do largely without the school! Only if the school succeeds in making itself dispensable does it perform its task properly of preparing the pupils for life. We usually refer to this process as 'promoting learner autonomy'. By 'promoting learner autonomy' we mean 'enabling the learners to increasingly take charge of their own learning'. Again, foreign-language teaching offers excellent opportunities for this. We have already seen how the choice of topics to be dealt with in the classroom may be negotiable. The communicative approach enables us to go much further, however. It is eminently suitable for giving the pupils insight into what they need to learn, into what they have learnt and what they still have to learn. It enables objectives, not only long-term objectives but even single-lesson objectives, to be stated in such a way that the pupils understand what they are doing and why they have to do it. It enables the pupils to monitor their own progress, not only on the basis of the teacher's approval or disapproval but because they themselves realize how far they have got, what they can do and what they cannot do yet. I remember being present during a lesson in a classroom in Germany where all the pupils (10–11 years old) had a list of what they – together with the teacher – had decided to learn and where they ticked off what they felt they could already do, happily going on to the next item because it was one more meaningful step to the achievement of their objective for that year. The items were specified in such understandable terms as 'introducing yourself', 'spelling your name', 'giving your telephone number', 'asking the way', 'showing the way', 'talking about pets', 'saying when something happened', etc. etc. In this classroom, from the first lesson onwards, the pupils were made to feel that they were participating in the decision-making process and had their own responsibility for learning what they had decided they wanted to learn – and, I should add, responsibility for helping others to achieve their aim as well. At the same time they were capable of monitoring their own progress and, if necessary, of influencing the conduct of each lesson. The role of the teacher in all this was, if anything, more important than in the traditional classroom. The teacher's role had changed from that of the authority 'who knows what is good for the children' into that of a guide, a counsellor. A more demanding role, it is true, but also an infinitely more satisfying one. In a recent report on experiments in Sweden, Salin notes that these have shown that it is possible to make students (the experiments concerned adult education but are certainly not without relevance to school education) 'more active and responsible for their learning'. 'Experiments with different forms of self-assessment', he goes on to say, 'have shown that the students are well capable of assessing their own proficiency, if they have had some training and use appropriate tools'. The overall result of the experiments is that 'the motivation has increased, there have been very few drop-outs and the results have improved in courses where the learners have had the possibility of influencing the contents of the course, the choice of materials and methods of work'. Surely it must be more satisfying for a teacher to work in such conditions than to be faced with the customary growth of indifference, boredom and rebellion. It must also be more satisfying for a teacher to realize that he or she is not only involved in just teaching a language but, what is more important, in helping the pupils to prepare themselves for life in our modern society. Adult life in a democratic society demands the ability and willingness to make decisions and to take responsibility, responsibility not only for one's own life but also for the affairs of the community. The attitudes and skills required for this are not guaranteed by a school-leaving certificate; they can only be the result of a long period of preparation, a preparation for which the school is largely responsible and in which every teacher has an important role to play.

We seem to have imperceptibly moved from one point of orientation to another, from the learner to society. It is a matter for political philosophy to discuss the question whether these two orientations coalesce, and if so to what extent. Suffice it to say here that it is in the interest of society that its members should be able to exploit their full potential for its benefit. The capacity for playing an adequate role in a democratic society is certainly a point of orientation for education in general and for foreign-language teaching in particular. The foreign-language teacher can – as we have seen – significantly contribute to the development of the learner into a responsible adult. Through the medium of the foreign language, the learner can also be intensively confronted with other cultures, other traditions, other modes of thinking. This confrontation, if handled properly and without bias, can provide the pupils with a wider understanding and a broader perspective than isolation in their own culture can ever give. It will, in turn, give them a deeper understanding of their own culture and in this way, too, prepare them for meaningfully participating in it.

Our final point of orientation – it would be unrealistic to ignore this – has to be the examination system. This is not the time and place to discuss advantages and disadvantages of examinations. Whether we like it or not, we would be neglecting our duty if we did not prepare our pupils for whatever examinations they may wish or have to take. In principle, preparing pupils for an examination need not conflict with any of the other tasks we have discussed. Whether it does or not depends on the nature of the examination itself. A valid examination test is an operationalization of the objectives of the learning programme and preparing pupils for such a test is therefore the same thing as helping them achieve their objectives. Unfortunately, as we all know, examination tests are certainly not always valid operationalizations of our objectives and even in the best cases they cover only part of our objectives. Yet passing examinations is undeniably a need of our pupils. If we accept this need there are two courses open to us, even if we see them only as making a virtue out of necessity. The two courses can be pursued simultaneously. On the one hand, if the content of an examination is inadequate in view of our objectives we can exert our influence to achieve a reform of the examination so that it validly reflects our objectives. On the other hand, even if the examination is inadequate, we can use every opportunity – and of course there are many such opportunities – to ensure that our pupils reach our more valid objectives in spite of it. In fact, it may often be the case that the best way to prepare our pupils for any language examination is to start by enabling them to acquire a general communicative ability anyway.

To sum up, the needs of our pupils in general education can be characterized as bridging the gap between what they are when entering the educational system and what they need to be when leaving school. In this perspective we have distinguished four orientations for the planning of learning programmes:

1. The subject, i.e. the achievement of communicative ability in a foreign language;
2. The learner, particularly the learner as a communicator, as a learner, and as an individual with a role in society;
3. Society, particularly democratic society;
4. The examination system.

Together, these four orientations give meaningful direction to our activities as teachers. As foreign-language teachers we have significant contributions to make in each direction. If we are to fulfil our role adequately we cannot afford to ignore even one of them.

COUNCIL
OF EUROPE

CONSEIL
DE L' EUROPE

3   CHAPTER THREE: 3

OBJECTIVES

INTRODUCTION TO CHAPTER THREE

Learning objectives play a major role in systems development. The first extract in this chapter describes this role, specifies the conditions to be fulfilled if objectives are to play this role adequately, and presents the first language-learning objective to be developed in the Project, the Threshold Level for adult language learning, exemplified for English. It also describes the way this objective has functioned in the Project and the developments it has given rise to.

This introductory extract is followed by a number of samples from *The Threshold Level*, exemplifying the ways in which the various descriptive categories are specified and elaborated in the definition of the objective. For the full specification the reader is referred to the volume from which the samples have been taken.

Extracts III.2.a–d present and exemplify *Waystage*, an objective approximately halfway between zero and Threshold Level. A comparison of some of these extracts with the corresponding ones from the Threshold Level will show how communicative objectives may be vertically differentiated.

Extract III.3 deals with the place of language-learning objectives in the perspective of more general educational objectives. It shows the close interdependence between the two types of objectives and explores the consequences of this interdependence for educational practice.

from J A. van Ek in: *Modern Languages (1971–1981)*

OBJECTIVES: THE THRESHOLD LEVEL

1. Unorganized and organized learning

Experientia docet. We live and learn. Living inevitably involves the undergoing of experiences and the undergoing of experiences inevitably changes us; it changes our modes of thinking, of judging, of behaving. If we regard thinking and judging as specific modes of behaviour, we may say that the undergoing of experiences changes our behaviour-potential. It enables us – although this does not always become manifest – to behave differently from the way we behaved before we underwent the experiences. The change in our behaviour-potential under the influence of experiences is what we usually refer to as *learning*.

Much of our learning is unorganized, unconscious and unintentional. It is simply a product of everyday living. Much of it, too, is hardly perceptible, especially if monotonous patterns and regular routines play predominant parts in our lives. Then the experiences we undergo fail to stimulate us and the impact is slight. However, we also – some of us more frequently than others – undergo more intensive experiences that may affect our behaviour-potential profoundly and permanently. Again, these experiences may be unorganized and unintentional – we live and learn – but we may also deliberately set out to change our behaviour-potential, to learn. Then learning is intentional and we will introduce some form of organization into the experiences we seek. This organization may be minimal. It may simply mean exposing ourselves to the natural circumstances under which the required behaviour is likely to develop, like jumping into the water in order to learn how to swim or moving into a foreign-language-speaking community in order to learn their language. Even then, however, we normally tend to adopt a somewhat less minimal form of organization. We will start by jumping into shallow water and perhaps look at others in order to see how they manage to remain afloat, and, in the foreign community, we will be especially looking for those experiences that seem to be most relevant to us. Moving up the scale of organization we may increasingly programme the experiences we expose ourselves to, hoping thus to achieve more efficient and more effective learning. The less natural the conditions under which our learning is to take place, the more beneficial such programming may seem to be. We may even seek the aid of professionals in the provision of learning-inducing experiences and more or less abandon our autonomy as learners. Formal education is characterized by a high degree of organization in the provision of learning-inducing experiences and often, though not invariably, by a low degree of learner-autonomy. This is particularly – some would say inevitably – true of mass education, where various constraints – notably economic ones – may even impose a certain degree of rigidity.

Organized learning may thus take place under many different degrees of organization, ranging from autonomous and almost random learning to fully teacher-dependent and strictly programmed learning. In practice there are many mixed forms of organization. Random learning may be built into the programmes of even the most strictly organized forms of education, such as for instance extensive reading practice in modern languages in – usually the higher forms of – secondary schools. Also, the individualization of learning programmes and the promotion of learner autonomy are increasingly sought after in – especially the more progressive – institutions for mass education.

2. Characteristics of organized learning

Whatever the degree of organization and whatever the degree of learner autonomy, organized learning is a goal-oriented activity. All types of organized learning have in common the fact that learning is deliberately undertaken to bring about a desired change in the learner's behaviour potential.

Organized learning also implies that those learning experiences are sought which are likely to produce the desired change, to bring the learner nearer to the goal.

This, in turn, leads to a consideration of the resources available to the learner – or which may be made available – that will enable him or her to undergo the required learning experiences.

Once these resources have been determined a selection will have to be made. In this selection special consideration will have to be given to the various characteristics of the learners, such as their previous experience, their learning skills, the available time, etc, and also to ways in which the various resources can be made to fit together and be interrelated so that they may be most fruitfully exploited.

Organized learning, then, implies some measure of systematic planning, a kind of planning sometimes referred to as systems development even though the term may have unintended technological associations.

It will be clear from the above discussion that organized learning is only possible if whoever does the organizing – whether the learner, a teacher or an organization – has some insight into the nature of the required change in behaviour potential, in other words into the learning goal. In organized learning, learning goals are always present, usually in the form of more or less specified learning aims or objectives. This does not mean that these objectives are always explicitly present or are always the result of conscious and deliberate planning. In the absence of such explicitly adopted and consciously planned objectives, teachers will often resort to those course materials which happen to be available, if not actually prescribed, and then the acquisition of the content of a course book may, intentionally or unintentionally, become the objective, whether it is directly related to the ultimate learning goal or not. However, if organized learning is to be optimally effective, carefully planned objectives are indispensable.

3. Roles of objectives

Objectives, as was argued above, give meaningful direction to the organization of learning. Indicating what the result of the learning is to be, they make possible a conscious selection of those learning experiences that are most likely to bring about the desired result. This includes the selection of learning methods and learning materials (course books, realia, sound tapes, etc). They also make an estimate possible of the time likely to be required in order to achieve the ultimate result. They make conscious decisions possible, but – and there should be no misunderstanding about this – they do not dictate such decisions. Of course, if the objective is the ability to read in a foreign language, much reading practice will be required, but the objective does not indicate to what extent, if any, this reading practice should be preceded or accompanied by independent grammar and/or vocabulary learning, whether explicit comparisons with the learners' native language should be made, etc, etc. Objectives, then, may be said to indicate certain activities that must be included, or even highlighted, in the learning procedure, but they do not, in themselves, lay down such a procedure.

Objectives can be distinguished into terminal objectives (those describing the intended end-result of the learning process) and intermediate objectives. Learning is a process evolving in time, and organized learning usually implies the distinction of a number of successive stages or steps towards the terminal objective. Each of these steps has its own – intermediate – objective. Intermediate objectives form part of the programming of the learning process and the recognition of such objectives contributes to the conscious planning of learning programmes. Intermediate objectives also play an important role in motivating the learners for the sustained effort that any learning task of longer duration requires. Particularly if the intermediate objectives are clearly related towards the terminal objective they enable the learners to take note of their own progress, providing them with the satisfaction that meaningful progress is being made.

The motivating role of objectives is not confined to intermediate objectives. It goes without saying that terminal objectives set up or chosen by the learners themselves also constitute a powerful source of motivation: they describe that which the learners wish to be able to do. However, imposed terminal objectives (often found in compulsory schooling) may also promote the learners' motivation, on the condition that they are recognized as valid and worthwhile.

The roles of objectives mentioned so far may be said to be *intrinsic* to organized learning. However, objectives may also play roles that are *extrinsic* to learning itself. These are roles related to the overall organization of educational systems and to the social recognition of successful learning.

In principle, educational systems – or school systems – are designed to provide society with the attitudes, knowledge and skills required for its existence and to provide the individual members of society with opportunities to fulfil their own potential. That these two aims may be – and often are – in conflict with each other does not detract from their basic validity, nor does it alter the fact that all educational systems try to fulfil at least one of them in a considerable measure and the other to a higher or a lower degree.

In order to make the achievement of these aims possible, educational systems are based on vertical and horizontal differentiation. The vertical differentiation concerns learning facilities – often provided in schools – at different levels, the horizontal differentiation concerns learning facilities at the same level but with different programmes. In an adequate educational system the various learning facilities are systematically related to each other. This means that vertical and horizontal transition from one learning facility (school, course, institution) to another can be made with minimal delay or loss and with maximal smoothness. In order to achieve this facility of transition, clearly defined objectives for each element of the educational system are indispensable.

Another reason why clearly defined objectives are essential in an educational system is that the achievement of an objective may carry considerable social advantages for the learners and that therefore recognition of successful learning should be given on the fairest and most objective basis possible. This fairness and objectivity can only be obtained if the learning-objectives are clearly specified, which is a precondition of reliable and valid assessment of the learners' achievements.

4. Some conditions for successful objectives

We regard objectives as successful if they are capable of fulfilling the roles described above.

The aim of learning is to change the learners' behaviour potential. Learning-objectives should reflect this aim and consequently specify *what the learners will be able to do* after having completed the learning process. In other words, objectives should be described in *behavioural* terms. *Behavioural objectives* are to be distinguished from the type of objectives current not long ago, which specified learning aims in terms such as 'the learner will know . . .', 'the learner will be familiar with . . .', etc, etc. Apart from leaving the question unanswered just what is meant by 'knowing' or 'being familiar with', such objectives do not reflect the true learning aim since they do not state what *use* the learners will be able to make of their knowledge of or familiarity with the matters specified.

Objectives should also be formulated as *explicitly* as possible. As long as objectives are only described vaguely and generally, several of the roles ascribed to them above cannot be fulfilled by them. Thus it is not sufficient to say that 'the learners will have an adequate oral command of a foreign language'. Such a description of low explicitness can be interpreted in hundreds of different ways. Ideally, an objective should be formulated in such a way that only one single interpretation is possible. However, it is not always feasible to develop such fully explicit objectives. A case in point is the problem of specifying the range of accents that learners will be able to cope with when listening to foreign language speakers. Even though accents themselves may be described objectively and accurately, they can never be included in an objective as independent parameters, since intelligibility is determined by numerous different parameters that may reinforce or counteract each other in ways that do not seem to lend themselves to objective description. Thus, for instance, a speaker using an accent widely deviating from the standard accent, but speaking clearly on a familiar subject, may be easier to understand than one using a standard or near-standard accent who speaks indistinctly and deals with an unfamiliar subject. Just how these, and many other, factors influence each other, and therefore overall intelligibility, is a question that has not been satisfactorily answered so far. If, then, total explicitness is usually not possible in, for instance, the description of foreign-language learning objectives, it should nevertheless be endeavoured to attain the highest possible degree of explicitness. One example of the provisional result of such an attempt will be dealt with below.

Another condition for successful objectives, the last one to be discussed here, is that they should have a high degree of *flexibility*. Even the most homogeneous groups of learners consist of individuals who differ from each other in background, learning skills, interests, motivation, etc. Whilst sometimes, especially for certification purposes, a certain uniformity may be required, objectives should be defined in such a way that they leave maximum scope for differences between individual learners. This means that they must be flexible enough to allow a high degree of learner-orientation. This flexibility may be achieved for instance by defining an objective hierarchically, ie at successive levels of delicacy, indicating at which levels the specified elements are optional or replaceable by other elements.

5. The threshold level

The 'threshold level' is an objective for foreign language learning based on a model for the description of such objectives which was developed in the framework of the Modern Languages Project of the Council for Cultural Co-operation of the Council of Europe. The model was designed for the development of objectives satisfying the conditions mentioned under 4 above and capable of fulfilling the roles discussed under 3. Thus the model leads to the specification of *behavioural* objectives with a high degree of *explicitness* and *flexibility*.

The English version, *The Threshold Level*, developed for adult learners, was the first language-learning objective to be published in which it was attempted to fulfil the conditions mentioned under **4** with full consistency. It has been, and still is, a major point of orientation of the Project Group's activities and, as the first concrete exemplification of the application of the principles underlying the Modern Languages Project, it has had a strong influence on developments in modern-language teaching generally. It did not start the trend towards more behaviourally oriented language teaching, but it strongly reinforced it by providing a basis for experimentation and course development that was not only more concrete but also more comprehensive and consistent than what had previously been available. Like some earlier objectives, *The Threshold Level* contains lists of words and grammatical structures that are recommended for acquisition by the learners in order to be able to function in the foreign language in the way specified elsewhere in the objective. It differs from earlier objectives, however, in that the selection of language forms (words and grammatical structures) is fully related to and directly derived from behavioural specifications. In other words, *The Threshold Level* is a detailed specification of what the learners will be able to *do* in the foreign language, with, in addition, recommendations as to which words and grammatical structures may most economically enable them to do what is specified in the main (behavioural) part of the objective.

A major concept underlying the threshold level is that one of the conditions for successful learning is that the learners should be aware that what they are learning is relevant to their own purposes. *The Threshold Level* therefore attempts to specify in what situations the members of the target group are most likely to wish to use the foreign language and what they will need to be able to do with the foreign language in those situations. The situations are characterized in terms of four components:

1. The *social roles* which the learner will be able to play;
2. The *psychological roles* which the learner will be able to play;

3. The *settings* in which the learner will be able to use the foreign language;
4. The *topics* which the learner will be able to deal with in the foreign language.

What the learners will be able to do in the various situations is described in general terms with regard to each topic (eg topic *health and welfare*, subtopic *ailments/accidents*: learners will be able to report illness, injury, accident; say whether they have been ill before and whether they have been operated upon; say whether they have to take medicine regularly, if so, what medicine) and more specifically in terms of *language functions* and *notions*. *Language functions* are what people do by means of language, eg *apologizing, requesting, expressing doubt*, etc. *Notions* are the concepts, and the relations between them, with regard to which people fulfil language functions, eg *absence* in *apologizing for absence*, *aid* in *requesting aid*, and *validity* and *ticket* as well as the relation between these two concepts in *expressing doubt about the validity of a ticket*. The *notions* are further subdivided into *general notions*, ie those likely to be expressed no matter what the topic (*absence, time-when, ownership*, etc.) and *specific*, ie more strictly topic-related, *notions* (topic *ailments/accidents*, specific notions: *ill, pain, fever, health*, etc.).

Finally, *The Threshold Level* describes *how well* people will be able to do all that has been specified; in other words, it describes the *degree of skill* required in order to do adequately all that has been specified.

The Threshold Level is the result of the application of a model for the description of language-learning objectives to a particular target group. In order to make the objective as widely useful as possible, that target group was selected which was felt to be the largest single group of potential adult learners in the member countries of the Council of Europe. The members of this group are characterized as follows:

1. They will be temporary visitors to the foreign country;
or
2. They will have temporary contacts with foreigners in their own country;
3. Their contacts with foreign language speakers will, on the whole, be of a superficial, non-professional type;
4. They will primarily need only a basic level of command of the foreign language.

The Threshold Level is an attempt to specify those linguistic abilities that are considered most likely to satisfy the estimated foreign-language needs of the members of this target group. The subjective element in the previous statement will be obvious: 'considered most likely', 'the estimated needs'. A similar subjectivity plays a role in the specifications themselves. It is present in the classification and selection of language functions, of general and specific notions, of topics, etc. It is also present in the selection of words and grammatical structures. In the author's view such subjectivity is inevitable in our present state of knowledge, a situation that is not likely to change in the foreseeable future. However, the successive decisions are not arbitrary or haphazard. They show a high degree of correspondence with decisions made by others for comparable target groups, and they have been checked, rechecked and approved by several consultants. The vocabulary lists, finally, were checked against existing selections and word-frequency lists, not in order to make them correspond to these lists but to make certain that no items were inadvertently overlooked. Yet it is not all that difficult for individual critics to find fault with certain decisions, to point out omissions, redundancies or inadequacies. This means there is room for improvement. That such improvements would be necessary was foreseen when *The Threshold Level* was published as — emphatically — a *provisional* specification. That some find it easy to suggest improvements would seem to indicate that the attempt to make a transparent, easily verifiable specification was successful.

The Threshold Level has a high degree of *explicitness*, but, for reasons discussed earlier (see **4**), it is not fully explicit. Full explicitness was not possible at the time when it was first developed, nor is it possible now. Yet, a further approach towards explicitness would seem to be feasible now notably in the areas of intonation as a means of realizing language functions, and of discourse structure, ie language structure above sentence level.

The *flexibility* of *The Threshold Level* is apparent and has meanwhile been widely exploited. The objective is defined in a set of interrelated components, several of which are hierarchically ordered at levels of increasing delicacy. At each level individual elements – together with the elements subordinated to them at levels of higher delicacy, if any – may, in principle, be lifted out of the specification and, if so desired, replaced by others that are more relevant to a particular target group or to individual learners. This flexibility was first exploited in *The Threshold Level for Modern Language Learning in Schools*, subsequently in various experimental applications of the objective, and it is currently exploited in the development of language-learning objectives for migrants.

The originality of the threshold level and of the principles underlying it — often associated with the so-called notional-functional approach – has been widely appreciated as a potential contribution to the solution of various present-day problems in language learning and teaching, notably problems related to motivation and to the individualization of learning.

The Threshold Level forms the basis for experimentation, innovation and, in some cases, curriculum reform in various European countries. In all the experiments a substantial increase of motivation (not only of the learners but also of the teachers) was established and in several cases *The Threshold Level* found a new application as a tool for successful teaching in mixed-ability groups. It owed its suitability for this purpose to the behavioural nature of the specifications. Especially the less demanding behavioural/functional tasks – those likely to be selected in the early stages of a learning programme – can soon be performed with at least minimal adequacy by practically all learners, irrespective of their learning ability, but the more gifted learners will perform them better (ie with a higher degree of formal correctness, with more variety and more subtlety) than others. This means, in effect, that all learners reach the same more general behavioural objectives (such as *asking the way, denying, apologizing*, etc), but that they differ as to their degree of skill. All learners, then, can successfully participate in the same classroom activities, but some will meanwhile learn more and perform better than others.

The experimentation referred to above has required the development of new course-materials reflecting the behavioural aim of language learning and incorporating the behavioural categories used in the objective. The approach underlying the threshold level proved to be so fundamentally different from earlier approaches that attempts at adapting existing materials were, on the whole, unsuccessful, so that completely new materials had to be designed.

Outside the controlled experiments, too, *The Threshold Level* has given a strong impetus to the development of new course materials. A great many courses recently published or now under preparation, especially for English as a foreign language but also for several other languages, are based on the functional-notional approach and, with or without explicit acknowledgement, exploit the specifications of *The Threshold Level*. This tendency is likely even to increase under the influence of the multi-media course *Follow Me*, which is now being broadcast in various countries. Directly based on *The Threshold Level*, this course is the result of co-operation between various organizations, including the Council for Cultural Co-operation of the Council of Europe, the BBC, the *Norddeutscher Rundfunk* and the *Bayerischer Rundfunk*, and the *Deutscher Volkshochschul-Verband*. Both the scale on which the course is used and the intensive teacher training that, in several countries, accompanies it will have a strong impact on language learning and teaching in a wide area.

6. Developments related to The Threshold Level

As was said before, *The Threshold Level* has served as a major point of orientation for the work of the Modern Languages Project Group of the Council of Europe.

It was used in the construction of a different objective for French, *Un niveau-seuil*, in which the same principles were applied but developed into a richer, more comprehensive, structure, resulting in an inventory from which early learning objectives might be derived for a variety of target groups, and incorporating a first approach to the elaboration of discourse structure.

The Threshold Level was the direct model for the development of comparable objectives for Spanish, German, Italian and Danish. The German version (*Kontaktschwelle*), though directly related to the original English version, contains numerous improvements partly based on experiences meanwhile gained in the implementation of *The Threshold Level* and on critical reactions.

The Threshold Level also formed the point of departure for the development of an objective for English called *Waystage*, which represents a halfway point for beginning learners whose ultimate objective is *The Threshold Level*. *Waystage* is meant as an example of how the total learning-load for *The Threshold Level* may be divided into a first stage and a second stage in a principled way. The need for such a halfway objective arose when the programme for the first year of the two-year multi-media course *Follow Me* (see above) had to be designed.

Finally, *The Threshold Level*, like *Un niveau-seuil*, is the basis for the development of objectives for other target groups. Notably on behalf of migrants various projects are in progress in several European countries.

Other activities of the Project Group that are directly related to *The Threshold Level* include test development, both in the field of self-assessment and in formal, objective testing. A specimen Threshold-Level test is now being used for experimental purposes.

7. The threshold level and methodology

Objectives do not impose a methodology. The threshold level may be reached by a variety of methods in a variety of different ways. Yet, since spontaneous (especially oral) communicative behaviour is the aim embodied in the threshold level, any successful method leading up to it will have to include ample practice in such behaviour. Whether grammar and translation practice and/or vocabulary memorization are part of the method or not is of secondary importance in comparison with the need to practise that which is specified in the objective.

Practising communicative behaviour is an important factor in promoting the learners' motivation. Asking learners to practise what they themselves recognize as their learning-aim makes sense to them, more than requiring them to engage in activities that only on the authority of the teacher or another expert can be accepted by them as ultimately leading up to the desired objective. It has already been established in experimentation that it is possible to make even the most naive learners realize the significance and validity of communicative learning aims and that it is possible as well to engage their full co-operation in preparing for such aims, provided the tasks they are asked to perform are transparently related to these aims. The transparency of this relation is a clue to learner participation and to insightful learning. Communicative aims, as has been proved in experimentation, can be presented in a way which is intelligible to practically all learners and it is equally possible to give learners insight into the steps leading up to these aims. Such insight is, of course, essential to another aspect of learner participation, the aspect of self-assessment, of the monitoring by the learners themselves of their own progress. The more successful course materials based on *The Threshold Level* make provisions for insightful learning and also offer the learners tools for the assessment of their progress.

Practice in genuine communicative behaviour, right from the start of the learning process, is also motivating because it gives the learners the confidence that, from the first lesson onwards, they can already do something that they recognize as part of their ultimate objective. It is important, of course, that this practice should be individualized as much as possible. Now and then learners may take pleasure in playing roles which are completely different from their own, but since their aim is to use the foreign language themselves, in their own capacity, they should get ample practice in doing just that. This means that a specification such as that of *The Threshold Level* should never be used as a prescriptive inventory of what the learner is 'allowed' to do. The various behavioural elements, and even more so the recommended words and grammatical structures, represent an estimate of the needs and interests of the *average* learner, an artificial concept. Since individual learners will always be different from this average learner, the specifications will inevitably never fit them exactly. Consequently they should be used as guidelines rather than a straightjacket, a recommendation which has, fortunately, proved to be superfluous for all those engaged in pilot experimentation in the framework of the Modern Languages Project of the Council of Europe.

The requirement that practice in genuine communicative behaviour should constitute a major element of the learning process right from the start imposes the need for functional grading on course materials. That this is the case has been recognized by course designers ever since *The Threshold Level* became available. Initially, however, serious doubts were expressed as to the feasibility of combining, or integrating, such functional grading with the structural grading that is generally felt to be essential for efficient language learning. The main effort of those who have designed course materials for threshold level has since been directed towards the solution of this problem. A variety of course materials now bears witness the successful outcome of this effort. The success is usually due to the introduction of the principle of recycling. This means that the various language functions re-occur in a course with more or less regular intervals, that on their first occurrence they are realized with linguistically simple means and that the linguistic apparatus with which they are fulfilled is made increasingly more complex at each subsequent occurrence.

8. Conclusion and outlook

With the development and publication of *The Threshold Level* the Council for Cultural Co-operation of the Council of Europe has made a significant contribution to the promotion of foreign-language learning as a basis for international understanding. *The Threshold Level* has generated numerous innovative developments in modern-language learning and teaching and, as a product of international co-operation, has stimulated intensive and fruitful interaction between those responsible, in whatever capacity, for language teaching in a large number of European countries. It has also contributed to educational innovation at a more general level by serving as an example of a tool that may effectively be used to promote learner-centred and needs-oriented teaching and to stimulate genuine learner participation, ultimately leading to learner autonomy.

Meanwhile, numerous activities – including pilot experiments – related to the threshold level provide the feedback required to maintain and further reinforce the international collaboration resulting from the Modern Languages Project. Several improvements in the present specifications have been suggested and will have to be carefully considered. The demand for further objectives, developed on the same basis, at different levels and for more languages, is continuous and persistent. The intensification and extension of interaction-networks is a major desideratum of all those concerned with the application of the principles of the Modern Languages Project. Above all, there is a need for international co-operation in the training of modern-language teachers. The effectiveness of the proposals made by the Project Group is to a large extent dependent on the ability of teachers to implement them. Their innovative nature requires not only special knowledge and skills on the part of the teachers, but especially an attitude consonant with the educational philosophy underlying them. Experience has proved that many teachers can be readily motivated to make the necessary adjustments. However, this has been confined so far to comparatively limited groups of teachers, often working under special conditions. An all-out international effort will be required in order to reach the stage where the proposals of the Project Group can be competently and successfully implemented on a large scale all over the area of the Council of Europe member countries.

INTRODUCTION TO EXTRACTS III.1.b–i

In the preceding extract (III.1.a) the model is described which was developed for the specification of language-learning objectives in the Modern Languages Project. The same extract introduces the Threshold Level and the ways in which the various descriptive categories of the model are used in the definition of this objective. The following extracts (III.1.b–i) present the actual definition of the *Threshold Level* in detail.

III.1.b deals with the specification of 'situations' and contains a small sample from the list of 'settings' as well as the full list of 'topics' used in the *Threshold Level*.

III.1.c contains a description of the objective in terms of 'the four skills'.

III.1.d presents the full list of 'language functions' in the *Threshold Level*.

III.1.e is a sample of the 'behavioural specifications' with regard to each 'topic'. It is part of a much longer specification but should suffice to give the reader an idea of how this component may be described.

III.1.f presents the full list of 'general notions' in the *Threshold Level*.

III.1.g, h and i are samples of the specifications of recommended language-forms ('exponents') for language functions, general notions and specific notions respectively.

from J A van Ek, *The Threshold Level/Threshold Level English*

5¹ SPECIFICATION OF SITUATIONS

By *situation* we mean the complex of extra-linguistic conditions which determines the nature of a language act (*cf* Chapter 2). Properly speaking, situations are strictly personal and unique. One of the conditions is always the individual language-user himself with his unique background (the sum total of his experiences). For our purposes, however – the definition of a level of general language ability will be an objective for a very large and heterogeneous population – we must ignore strictly individual conditions and we may concentrate on four components of situations, which, together, provide a sufficient basis for the further steps in our procedure. We shall henceforward, distinguish four components of situations:

1. the *social roles* which the learner will be able to play;
2. the *psychological roles* which the learner will be able to play;
3. the *settings* in which the learner will be able to use the foreign language;
4. the *topics* which the learner will be able to deal with in the foreign language.

Social roles

The principal social roles for which T-level learners have to be prepared are:

1. *stranger/stranger*;
2. *friend/friend*.

This selection is made from a study by Richterich (1972) *A model for the definition of language needs of adults learning a modern language*, on the basis of the characteristics of the target-group (*cf* Chapter 4). Various other roles are subsumed under 1, eg:

private person/official
patient/doctor, nurse, dentist.

A role such as

asker/giver

may be subsumed under both 1 and 2.

The inclusion of role 2 (friend/friend) has important consequences for the definition of the T-level. It raises this level above that required for purely physical survival in a foreign-language environment. It will prepare the learner for the establishment and maintenance of social relationships with foreign-language speakers. Only when this need is fulfilled can our level be called 'threshold level' in a meaningful way: it will enable the learner to cross the threshold into the foreign-language community.

Psychological roles

On the basis of the characteristics of the target group we select from Richterich (*op cit*) the following roles:

---

[1] Chapter numbers are those of the source volume. References to chapters in the text are also the original ones. (Ed.)

1. neutrality
2. equality
3. sympathy
4. antipathy.

These roles are the more 'neutral' roles and they are appropriate in a large variety of types of linguistic interaction.

Settings[2]

On the basis of the characteristics of the target group, we may draw up a long list of settings in which the learners may want to use the foreign language. The settings have been selected from lists provided by Richterich (*op cit*) and by Peck (private communication). In spite of its size this list is not to be considered exhaustive. It is assumed, however, that it is sufficiently comprehensive to produce – together with the other components of situation – specifications of language-ability which will enable the learners to behave adequately also in various settings which have not been listed (transfer).

1. Geographical location
1. foreign country where foreign language is native language
2. foreign country where foreign language is not native language
3. own country.

2. Place

2.1 Outdoors
1. street
2. square
3. park, garden
4. terrace
5. countryside
6. beach
7. lake, sea
8. mountains
9. sports-field
10. open air swimming pool
11. camping site
12. bus stop
13. taxi stand
14. sights
15. market-place
16. car-park.

2.2 Indoors

2.2.1 Private life
1. house
2. apartment
3. room
4. kitchen.

[2] Sample (Ed.).

Topics

On the basis of the characteristics of the target-group, the following list of topics has been drawn up. A similar list provided by Peck has been used as the main source. In the composition of the list the social roles we have selected have been used as criteria for inclusion. With respect to this list the same remark applies which was made apropos of the list of settings: a certain measure of arbitrariness in the classification does not affect the value of the list as long as all the more important topics are included somewhere. Even this claim, however, cannot be upheld. No matter how carefully a list of this kind is composed, it is bound to be far from complete. However, this weakness is – to a certain extent – offset by the transfer-potential of linguistic ability. It may be assumed that a learner who is competent to deal with the topics listed will also be able to deal with several other topics for which he has not necessarily been prepared.

1. Personal identification

1.1 name
1.2 address
1.3 telephone number
1.4 date and place of birth
1.5 age
1.6 sex
1.7 marital status
1.8 nationality
1.9 origin
1.10 profession, occupation
1.11 employer
1.12 family
1.13 religion
1.14 likes and dislikes
1.15 character, temperament, disposition.

2. House and home

2.1 types of accommodation
2.2 accommodation, rooms
2.3 furniture, bedclothes
2.4 rent
2.5 services
2.6 amenities
2.7 region
2.8 flora and fauna.

3. Trade, profession, occupation

3.1 trades, professions, occupations
3.2 place of work
3.3 conditions of work
3.4 income

3.5 training
3.6 prospects.

4. Free time, entertainment

4.1 hobbies
4.2 interests
4.3 radio, TV, etc
4.4 cinema, theatre, opera, concert, etc
4.5 sports
4.6 intellectual pursuits
4.7 artistic pursuits
4.8 museums, galleries, exhibitions
4.9 press.

5. Travel

5.1 travel to work, evening-class, etc
5.2 holidays
5.3 countries and places
5.4 public transport
5.5 private transport
5.6 entering and leaving a country
5.7 nationalities
5.8 languages
5.9 hotel, camping-site, etc
5.10 travel documents
5.11 fares
5.12 tickets
5.13 luggage
5.14 traffic.

6. Relations with other people

6.1 friendship/aversion
6.2 invitations
6.3 correspondence
6.4 club-membership
6.5 political and social views.

7. Health and welfare

7.1 parts of the body
7.2 positions of the body
7.3 ailments/accidents
7.4 personal comfort
7.5 sensory perception
7.6 hygiene
7.7 insurance
7.8 medical services
7.9 emergency services.

8. *Education*

8.1 schooling
8.2 subjects
8.3 qualifications.

9. *Shopping*

9.1 shopping-facilities
9.2 foodstuffs
9.3 clothes, fashion
9.4 smoking
9.5 household-articles
9.6 medicine
9.7 prices
9.8 weights and measurements.

10. *Food and drink*

10.1 types of food and drink
10.2 eating and drinking out.

11. *Services*

11.1 post
11.2 telephone
11.3 telegraph
11.4 bank
11.5 police
11.6 hospital, surgery, etc
11.7 repairs
11.8 garage
11.9 petrol-station.

12. *Places*

13. *Foreign language*

13.1 ability
13.2 understanding
13.3 correctness.

14. *Weather*

climate
weather-conditions.

6. LANGUAGE ACTIVITIES

From the characteristics of the target group and the situational specification of Chapter 5 we may conclude that the learners' need to use the foreign language orally will be much greater than their need to use its written forms. We even assume that, in the situations described, the members of the target group do not actually need a general ability to read and to write the foreign language. The threshold level, therefore, is essentially a level of oral communicative ability.

Oral communication may be one-sided, for instance, when one addresses an audience or listens to the radio. In most cases, however, especially in the situations specified for T-level, it will be an interaction process involving at least two people who speak and listen alternately.

The most important language activity for T-level learners is carrying on a conversation. This involves two skills: speaking and understanding. It will be obvious that the learners will have to be able to understand much more than they can say themselves. They can try to express themselves within the limitations of their linguistic command, but they have no such control over what is said to them by others. We can specify with some confidence the ability they will need in order to initiate a conversation on the topics listed, to get things done for them, or to fulfil other language functions. We can only guess at the ability they will need in order to react adequately when others initiate a conversation or respond to their own language acts. Even if we take into account – as we must – the efforts a native speaker will make in order to make himself understood by a foreigner with only a basic level of command of his language, we shall have to provide the learner with a fairly great receptive ability if he is to maintain himself in a conversation at all. Exactly what the learner will be able to do in the foreign language at T-level is specified in detail in the following chapters. It may be useful to give a brief summary here of what this implies for the skill of *understanding*:

The learners will be able to understand:

– the most likely answers to questions asked by themselves;
– the most likely responses to matters raised by themselves or to answers given by themselves;
– questions asked by others within the topic areas listed in Chapter 5;
– information given by others within the topic areas listed in Chapter 5;
– the texts of the commonest announcements via public address systems in airports, at railway-stations, etc;
– warnings such as 'look out', 'be careful', 'stop!', 'hurry!'.

At this level the learners will be expected to understand only those utterances which are spoken in the standard dialect with either the standard accent or accents which have a slight regional, foreign, and/or socio-economic colouring and at a speech-rate which lies in the lower range of what is considered normal.

The objective for *writing* at T-level is extremely limited. It is assumed that for this skill the actual needs of the majority of the members of the target-group do not go beyond the ability to write letters of one particular type and to fill in certain forms. This means, in fact, that no general ability to write is required but only a strictly limited formulaic manner of expression. The estimated needs of the learners can be listed as follows:

The learners will be able to write letters:

– inquiring about availability of accommodation (hotel, camping-site, etc);
– inquiring about price and conditions of accommodation;
– stating wishes as to size of rooms, arrangement (full board, etc), amenities, view;
– inquiring about tourist-attractions, sights, etc,
– booking accommodation.

The learners will be able to complete forms:

– hotel registration forms;
– forms required when entering or leaving the foreign country (if any).

The objective for *reading* is also narrowly restricted. At T-level the learners will be able to read:

– typewritten letters and simple brochures sent in return for letters written by the learners themselves (see under 'writing' above);
– generally used texts on road-signs;
– generally used public notices and announcements;
– generally used menu terms.

It should be emphasized that the above specifications for writing and reading constitute a minimum objective as derived from estimated needs at T-level. It is possible, and even likely, that courses meant for a literate target group will make extensive use of written forms of the language, not necessarily as part of the course objective, but as a teaching aid. It is also likely that the learners themselves, during the learning process, will utilize additional written materials in order to increase their language ability and/or for recreational purposes. It may be expected, therefore, that on reaching T-level the majority of learners will have a much more general ability to use the written forms of the language – especially receptively – than what has been described in the objective. It is also possible that many learners will wish to follow up by means of correspondence social contacts which they have established orally with foreign-language speakers. These learners will need a more general ability to write the foreign language. On the other hand it should be recognized that a large section of the target group will not regard this as their primary objective. It would be contrary to the principles of the unit/credit system to force these learners to master this further ability before their general oral ability could be recognized. Both categories of learners should be accommodated in the unit/credit system, those who need only a strictly limited ability to use written forms of the language and those who wish to acquire a more general ability in reading alone or in reading and writing. It has therefore been decided to define the T-level in the way described in this study so with a general ability in speaking and understanding and a strictly limited ability in reading and writing, and to develop at a later stage two additional units, one for reading and one for writing, which in level and scope will correspond roughly to oral ability at T-level.

7. LANGUAGE FUNCTIONS

This chapter specifies component 3 of the definition of the T-level. This will be done in non-language-specific terms: we shall list the various functions the learners will be able to fulfil at T-level, whatever language – here limited to those spoken in the member-countries of the Council of Europe – they have studied. In Chapter 11 we shall list for each function the actual language forms (grammatical and/or lexical) which we consider to be the most useful exponents for T-level English.

In setting up our list of language functions we have distinguished six main categories of verbal communication:

1. imparting and seeking factual information;
2. expressing and finding out intellectual attitudes;
3. expressing and finding out emotional attitudes;
4. expressing and finding out moral attitudes;
5. getting things done (suasion);
6. socializing.

Each of these six main categories, and, indeed, each of the functions, may be realized separately in language acts. Often, however, two or more of them will be combined in a single language act. Thus, one may seek factual information while at the same time expressing surprise (emotional attitude). Yet, it is convenient to deal with each function separately and to specify just what each function involves by way of language content.

The list of functions is far from exhaustive. In the first place it is unlikely that it is possible at all to draw up a complete list. Secondly, the list represents a deliberate selection for T-level. At higher levels more functions would be added.

It should be emphasized that the lists presented here and in other chapters are not to be regarded as final or definitive. They will – it is hoped – provide a sufficiently solid basis for practical applications of an experimental nature. The feedback from this experimental work will undoubtedly lead to numerous modifications in the lists.

Language functions for T-level

1. Imparting and seeking factual information

1.1 identifying
1.2 reporting (including describing and narrating)
1.3 correcting
1.4 asking.

2. Expressing and finding out intellectual attitudes

2.1 expressing agreement and disagreement
2.2 inquiring about agreement or disagreement
2.3 denying something

2.4   accepting an offer or invitation
2.5   declining an offer or invitation
2.6   inquiring whether offer or invitation is accepted or declined
2.7   offering to do something
2.8   stating whether one remembers or has forgotten something or someone
2.9   inquiring whether someone remembers or has forgotten something or someone
2.10 expressing whether something is considered possible or impossible
2.11 inquiring whether something is considered possible or impossible
2.12 expressing capability and incapability
2.13 inquiring about capability or incapability
2.14 expressing whether something is considered a logical conclusion (deduction)
2.15 inquiring whether something is considered a logical conclusion (deduction)
2.16 expressing how certain/uncertain one is of something
2.17 inquiring how certain/uncertain others are of something
2.18 expressing one is/is not obliged to do something
2.19 inquiring whether one is obliged to do something
2.20 expressing others are/are not obliged to do something
2.21 inquiring whether others are obliged to do something
2.22 giving and seeking permission to do something
2.23 inquiring whether others have permission to do something
2.24 stating that permission is withheld.

3. Expressing and finding out emotional attitudes

3.1   expressing pleasure, liking
3.2   expressing displeasure, dislike
3.3   inquiring about pleasure, liking, displeasure, dislike
3.4   expressing surprise
3.5   expressing hope
3.6   expressing satisfaction
3.7   expressing dissatisfaction
3.8   inquiring about satisfaction or dissatisfaction
3.9   expressing disappointment
3.10 expressing fear or worry
3.11 inquiring about fear or worry
3.12 expressing preference
3.13 inquiring about preference
3.14 expressing gratitude
3.15 expressing sympathy
3.16 expressing intention
3.17 inquiring about intention
3.18 expressing want, desire
3.19 inquiring about want, desire.

4. Expressing and finding out moral attitudes

4.1   apologizing
4.2   granting forgiveness
4.3   expressing approval
4.4   expressing disapproval

4.5   inquiring about approval or disapproval
4.6   expressing appreciation
4.7   expressing regret
4.8   expressing indifference.

5. Getting things done (suasion)

5.1   suggesting a course of action (including the speaker)
5.2   requesting others to do something
5.3   inviting others to do something
5.4   advising others to do something
5.5   warning others to take care or to refrain from doing something
5.6   instructing or directing others to do something.

6. Socializing

6.1   to greet people
6.2   when meeting people
6.3   when introducing people and when being introduced
6.4   when taking leave
6.5   to attract attention
6.6   to propose a toast
6.7   when beginning a meal.

8. TOPICS: BEHAVIOURAL SPECIFICATIONS[3]

This chapter is a statement of what the learners will be able to do at T-level with respect to each of the topics listed in Chapter 5. The specification is non-language-specific and will serve as a basis for the notional specification discussed in Chapter 10.

1. Personal identification

Learners should be able to give and seek information about themselves and, if applicable, others, with regard to:

1.1	name	first name, initials, surname, spelling them out if required
1.2	address	home address, spelling it out if required
1.3	telephone number	
1.4	date and place of birth	spelling out the place-name if required
1.5	age	
1.6	sex	
1.7	marital status	
1.8	nationality	
1.9	origin	
1.10	profession, occupation	
1.11	employer	name of firm, company, institution, organization or individual by whom employed, nature of firm, company, institution or organization
1.12	family	composition of family, family-relations
1.13	religion	name of religion
1.14	likes and dislikes	especially with regard to people, hobbies and interests, food and drink
1.15	character, temperament, disposition	general characterization of other people.

2. House and home

Learners should be able to discuss where and under what conditions they and others live, specifically:

2.1	types of accommodation	describe the type of house, flat etc in which they live themselves, as well as those in the neighbourhood, seek similar information from others
2.2	accommodation, rooms	describe their own accommodation, house, flat, etc, and the rooms in it, seek similar information from others
2.3	furniture, bedclothes	mention and inquire about the availability of the most essential pieces of furniture and bedclothes

[3] Sample (Ed.).

2.4	*rent*	state, rent and/or purchase price of their own accommodation and inquire about that of other houses, flats, etc
2.5	*services*	mention and inquire about availability of such services as gas, electricity, heating, telephone
2.6	*amenities*	mention and inquire about availability of bath, shower, fridge, TV, garage, garden, cleaning facilities etc
2.7	*region*	characterize and inquire about the nature of their own region and that of others: agricultural, industrial, scenery, whether it is attractive or not etc
2.8	*flora and fauna*	characterize and inquire about flora and fauna of their own region and that of others.

3. Trade, profession, occupation

Learners should be able to exchange information about:

3.1	*trades, professions, occupations*	the nature of their own former and present jobs and those of others
3.2	*place of work*	where they and others work
3.3	*conditions of work*	working hours, holidays, position in an organization, employment and unemployment
3.4	*income*	income and taxation
3.5	*training*	the nature of training (if any) required for their own job and those of others
3.6	*prospects*	possibilities for further career, wishes and plans for future.

4. Free time, entertainment

Learners should be able to exchange information about:

4.1	*hobbies*	say what their hobbies are and inquire about those of others
4.2	*interests*	say what their special interests are and inquire about those of others
4.3	*radio, TV*	say whether they like watching TV, listening to the radio, which programmes they like particularly, which they dislike, and inquire about the preference of others
4.4	*cinema, theatre, opera, concert, etc*	state own preferences and inquire about those of others, inquire about programmes and booking facilities, buy tickets, ask for the cloakroom, find their way
4.5	*sports*	state own preferences and inquire about those of others, inquire about sporting

		events, buy tickets for stadium etc, discuss result of a match
4.6	*intellectual pursuits*	say whether they like reading and studying, whether they are actually studying, if so, what; seek similar information from others
4.7	*artistic pursuits*	say what forms of art they are interested in, if any; inquire about the preferences of others, give and seek information on the availability of public facilities: cinemas, theatre, museums etc
4.8	*museums, galleries, exhibitions*	say whether they are interested in museums, galleries, exhibitions; inquire about the interests of others; give and seek information on availability, price of tickets, opening-hours etc
4.9	*press*	say what they read regularly: newspapers, magazines etc; inquire about the preferences of others; inquire about the press in the foreign country.

5. Travel

The learners should be able to deal with various aspects of travelling:

5.1	*travel to work, evening-class etc*	say how they travel to work, evening-class, etc, what means of transport, what times, duration of journey, how often; seek similar information from others
5.2	*holidays*	say and inquire about where they and others normally spend their holidays and how long they last, how they spend them (camping, in hotels, etc), with whom (friends, relatives, etc); describe a previous holiday, where they went, how, with whom, for how long, where they stayed, what the weather was like, what they saw, what they did, give their general impressions and say whether they enjoyed the holiday and would go again; describe their plans for a future holiday and seek similar information from others; say whether they have been in the foreign-language country before, seek similar information from foreigners with respect to their own country; say which foreign country (countries) they would particularly like to visit and why; seek similar information from others

9. GENERAL NOTIONS

Notions are the concepts which people use in verbal communication. Such notions are heterogeneous in that they represent a wide variety of levels of abstraction. This is inevitable because it reflects the nature of language itself. We use language to refer to concrete objects such as chairs and tables, but we also use it to deal with highly abstract relations such as dative and objective relations. The list to be presented in this chapter is arranged systematically in accordance with the overall categorization proposed in Chapter 2. There is a considerable amount of overlap between this list and the lists in Chapter 7 and Chapter 10. Thus, for instance, the 'general notion' *capacity/incapacity* (2.4.3.10) is to a certain extent parallelled by the 'language function' *expressing capability and incapability*, and the 'general notion' *colour* (2.4.1.12) by 'specific' colour notions in the list described in Chapter 10. From a theoretical point of view, this may be unsatisfactory. It reflects our inability to deal with the question of 'what is done by means of language' in a strictly scientific way. What we have attempted, instead, was to develop a system of classification which, in spite of its shortcomings, would ensure the fullest possible coverage. This system is to a certain extent uneconomical in that it lists a number of items twice or even three times. From a practical point of view, however, this is hardly a disadvantage.

General notions

1. *Notions of entities*
including *Deixis* (see Chapter 11, division II)

2. *Notions of properties and qualities*

2.1	*Existential*	
2.1.1	existence/non-existence	
2.1.2	presence/absence	
2.1.3	availability/non-availability	
2.1.4	possibility/impossibility (objective)	
2.1.5	occurrence/non-occurrence	
2.2	*Spatial and temporal*	
2.2.1	location	
2.2.2	motion	
2.2.3	dimension	
	2.2.3.1	size
	2.2.3.2	length
	2.2.3.3	pressure
	2.2.3.4	weight
	2.2.3.5	volume
	2.2.3.6	temperature
	2.2.3.7	age
2.2.4	point of time	
2.2.5	length of time (duration)	
2.2.6	speed	

3. Notions of relations

3.1	*Spatial relations*
3.1.1	relative position
3.1.2	distance
3.1.3	direction
3.1.4	origin
3.1.5	arrangement

3.2	*Temporal relations*
3.2.1	priority
3.2.2	posteriority
3.2.3	sequence
3.2.4	simultaneousness
3.2.5	future reference
3.2.6	present reference
3.2.7	past reference
3.2.8	reference without time-focus
3.2.9	delay
3.2.10	earliness
3.2.11	lateness

3.3	*Action/event relations*
3.3.1	agency
3.3.2	objective (including factitive)
3.3.3	dative
3.3.4	instrumental
3.3.5	benefactive
3.3.6	place
3.3.7	time
3.3.8	manner, means

3.4	*Contrastive relations*
3.4.1	equality/inequality
3.4.2	correspondence/contrast

3.5	*Possessive relations*
3.5.1	ownership

3.6	*Logical relations*
3.6.1	conjunction
3.6.2	disjunction
3.6.3	inclusion/exclusion
3.6.4	cause
3.6.5	effect
3.6.6	reason
3.6.7	purpose
3.6.8	condition
3.6.9	focussing

Extract III.1.g

Content specification: Division I[4]

Language functions with T-level exponents for English[5]

1. Imparting and seeking factual information

1.1	*identifying*	demonstrative pronouns (*this, that, these, those*) + BE + NP P
		demonstrative adjectives (*this, that, these, those*) + N + BE + NP P
		personal pronouns (subject form) + BE + NP P
		declarative sentences P
		short answers (*Yes, he is*, etc) P
1.2	*reporting (including describing and narrating)*	declarative sentences P
		head-clause containing verb of saying (eg *to say*), thinking, etc + complement clause (indirect speech) P
1.3	*correcting*	same exponents as above; in addition:
		adverb *no* P
		negative sentences with *not* P
		sentences containing the negation-words *never, no* (adjective), *nobody, nothing* P
1.4	*asking*	interrogative sentences (yes/no questions) P
		declarative sentences + question intonation R
		question-word sentences with:

When
Where
Why
What (pronoun)
Which (pronoun)
Who
What (adjective)
Which (adjective)

How + { far, much, long, etc }

} P

[4] Sample (Ed.).

[5] Exponents marked R are meant for receptive use only: the learners will have to be able to understand them when others use them. Those marked P are meant for receptive and productive use: they are recommended as the most general and/or simplest way of fulfilling a language function or expressing a notion in speaking and, in rare cases, in writing.

Whose (pronoun and adjective) R
question-tags (type: You aren't afraid, are you) R

Tell me + $\dfrac{\text{(sub-clause)}}{\text{(about + NP)}}$ P

2. *Expressing and finding out intellectual attitudes*

2.1	*expressing agreement and dis-agreement*	
	agreement	I agree P
		That's right P
		Of course (not) P
		Yes P
		Certainly R
		affirmative short answers (it is, I am, I can, he may, etc) P
	disagreement	I don't agree P
		I don't think so P
		No P
		That's incorrect R
		negative short answers P
2.2	*inquiring about agreement or disagreement*	Do you agree? P
		Do you think so, too? P
		Don't you agree? P
		Don't you think so? P
		short questions P
2.3	*denying something*	No (adverb) P
		negative sentences with *not* P
		sentences containing the negation words *never, no* (adjective), *nobody, nothing* P
		negative short answers
2.4	*accepting an offer or invitation*	Thank you P
		Yes, please P
		I shall be very glad V_{to} ... P
		That will be very nice P
		With pleasure! R
2.5	*declining an offer or invitation*	No, thank you P
		I'm afraid I cannot ... P
		Unfortunately I cannot ... R
2.6	*inquiring whether offer or invitation is accepted or declined*	Will you + VP (do it, come, etc) P
2.7	*offering to do something*	Can I + VP P
		Shall I + VP P

2.8	*stating whether one remembers or has forgotten something or someone*	I remember ⎫ ⎧ noun(-group)/pronoun P I don't remember ⎭ + ⎨ gerund P ⎩ *that*-clause P I have forgotten (to bring my glasses etc) P

2.9	*inquiring whether someone remembers or has forgotten something or someone*	⎧ noun(-group)/
		Do you remember + ⎨ pronoun P
		                 ⎨ gerund P
		                 ⎩ *that*-clause P
		Have you forgotten to (bring your glasses, etc) P

2.10	*expressing whether something is considered possible or impossible* possibility	 ⎧ ø P It is possible + ⎨ *that*-clause P NP + can + VP P
	impossibility	It is not possible + *that*-clause P NP + cannot + VP P It is impossible P
2.11	*inquiring whether something is considered possible or impossible*	⎧ ø P Is it possible + ⎨ *that*-clause P Can + NP + VP P
2.12	*expressing capability and incapability*	Np + can + VP P NP + cannot + VP P NP + BE able to + VP P NP + BE not able to + VP P NP + BE unable to + VP R
2.13	*inquiring about capability or incapability*	Can + NP + VP P Cannot + NP + VP P BE + NP + able to + VP P BE not + NP + able to + VP P BE + NP + unable to + VP R
2.14	*expressing whether something is considered a logical conclusion (deduction)*	So + declarative sentence P Therefore + declarative sentence R NP + must + VP P *necessarily* in declarative sentence R NP + cannot + VP P
2.15	*inquiring whether something is considered a logical conclusion (deduction)*	*necessarily* in interrogative sentence R

Extract III.1.h

Content specification: Division II[6]

General notions with T-Level exponents for English

1. Notions of entities

the nominal and verbal entries in the lists of notions of Division III (specific notions)	*1. lexical exponents:* see the exponents of these notions in Division III.

2. *grammatical exponents:* deixis[7]

(A) *definite:*

  (a) non-anaphoric:

    personal pronouns (subject forms and object forms) P

    possessive adjectives (*my, your, their,* etc) P

    possessive pronouns (*mine, yours, theirs,* etc) as complement P
    This is mine

    possessive pronouns as subject R
    Mine is better

    demonstrative adjectives (attributive *this, these, that, those, such*) P

    demonstrative pronouns (independent *this, these, that, those*) P

    independent relative pronoun *what* P

    definite article *the* P

    interrogative pronouns (independent): *who* P, *whom* R, *whose* R, *what* P, *which* P

    interrogative adjectives (attributive): *whose* R, *what* P, *which* P

  (b) anaphoric:

    personal pronouns (subject forms and object forms) P

    possessive adjectives P

    possessive pronouns as complement P
    You take it; it is yours

    demonstrative adjectives P

---

[6] Sample (Ed.).

[7] *Deixis* is the grammatical system used for referring or identifying by means of linguistic items belonging to closed sets. Deixis may be *definite* or *indefinite* (**he** vs **someone**), *non-anaphoric* or *anaphoric* (*Why don't **you** come?* vs *I'll buy those books because I need **them***), *independent* or *attributive* (*I want **that*** vs *I want **that** book*). Deixis is not referentially restricted to entities; it may also be used for instance, for spatial and temporal qualities. Deictic exponents for each type of notions will be given in the appropriate places.

demonstrative pronouns P

relative pronouns: *who* P, *whose* R, *whom* R, *which* P, *that* R, ø R

emphatic pronouns: myself, yourself etc R

I've done it myself

definite article *the* P

adverbial *so* (as in: He wanted to leave, but he didn't say *so*) P

propword *one* (as in: I like the red one better) P

substitute-verb *do* (as in: He asked me to help him and I did) P

(B) *indefinite:*

indefinite article *a* P

indefinite pronouns:

someone P

somebody P

no-one P

(not ...) anybody P

(not ...) anyone P

nobody P

each P

everybody P

everyone P

something P

(not ...) anything P

nothing P

everything P

all (as in: They all went home; and in: I want all of it) P

both (as in: They both went home; and in: I want both of them) P

some (as in: Some of them went home) P

it (as in: It's raining) P

you (as in: It is a nice record if you like modern music) P

indefinite semi-deictics:

person R

There are five persons present

man (human beings) R

There were animals here before man came

people P

What do people think about the government?

There are five people present

thing P

What do you call that thing?

2. Notions of properties and qualities

2.1   *Existential*

2.1.1	existence/non-existence	There is ... P There's no ... P Is there ...? P to exist P

2.1.2	presence/absence	here P not here P away P

2.1.3	availability/non-availability	to have P ⎫ used in affirmative and to have got P ⎭ in negative contexts There is ... P There's no ... P Is there ...? P

2.1.4	possibility/impossibility (objective)	possible ⎫ impossible ⎬ P (see Division I, 2.10) can ⎪ cannot ⎭

2.1.5	occurrence/non-occurrence	to happen P

2.2   *Spatial and temporal*

2.2.1	location	here P there P somewhere P (not ...) anywhere P nowhere P where? P inside P *Put the car inside* outside P *The children are playing outside* everywhere P demonstrative adjectives ⎱ *this, that,* ⎱P demonstrative pronouns ⎰ *these, those*⎰ (see further Division II 3.1)

2.2.2	motion	to move P *The car did not move* to stand still R

to stop P
The car stopped suddenly
to go P
The car would not go
Why did you go?
to go + prepositional adjuncts of place P
He went to London
He went into the house
(see for further prepositions Division II, 3.1)
to go home P
to go away P
to go out P
to leave P
We left the station at ten o'clock
to arrive P
The train arrived at eleven o'clock
to come P
He came very late
He came to our house
to come along R
Why don't you come along?

Extract III.1.i

Content-specification: Division III[8]

Specific notions derived from topics and their T-level exponents for English

1. Personal identification

1.1	*name*	
	name	name P
		What's your name?
	forename	first name P
		Christian name R
		forename R
		His first name is Charles
	surname	surname P
		family name R
		His surname is Robinson
	initials	initials R
		Are your initials G B S?
	Mr (+ proper name)	Mr P
		This is Mr Jones
	Mrs (+ proper name)	Mrs P
		This is Mrs Jones
	Miss (+ proper name)	Miss P
		This is Miss Jones
	terms of address if no proper name is used (French: *monsieur, madame, mademoiselle*, as in *merci beaucoup, monsieur*)	No English exponents at T-level
	to spell	to spell P
		Can you spell your name, please?
	names of letters of the alphabet	a, b, c, etc. P
		z: [zed] or [zi:] P, the other pronunciation R
		My name is spelt b-l-a-c-k
	to call (= to refer to by the name of ...)	to call P
		We call him Pete
	to be called (= be referred to by the name of ...)	to be called P
		He is called Pete
	to sign (= to write one's signature)	to sign R
		Have you signed your cheque?
	signature	signature R
		Before we can pay this cheque we must have your signature
	letter (G *Buchstabe*)	letter P
		What is the last letter of your name?
1.2	*address*	
	address (= place of resi-	address P

[8] Sample (Ed.).

109

dence)	*What is your address?*
	My address is 15 Church Road, Cricklewood
to live (= to be domiciled)	to live P
	Where do you live?
	I live in France
street	street P
road	road P
square	square P
	I live in Portman Square
park	park P
	My house is near Hyde Park
house number	number P
	I live at number 15
	cardinal numerals up to four digits P
countries	country P
	names of own country, country (major countries)
	of foreign language, neighbouring countries of
	own country P
	neighbouring countries of foreign language coun-
	try R

1.3	*telephone number*	
	(see also 11.2)	
	telephone	telephone P
		phone R
		Have you got a telephone?
	to telephone	to telephone P[9]
		to call R
		to ring up R
		to make a (phone-)call R
		I'll call you at five o'clock
	telephone number	telephone number P
		cardinal numerals of 1 digit, including 0 P

1.4	*date and place of birth*	
	to be born	to be born P
		I was born in 1925
	place (G *Ort*, F *lieu*)	place P[10]
	birth	birth R
	date (= indication day, month, year)	date P

[9] This exponent is chosen for productive use because it constitutes the smallest additional learning load if the noun *telephone* has been learned, moreover it is the most 'international' of the exponents.

[10] In language communication situations the combination of the notions 'birth' and 'place' will have several exponents, such as 'What is your *birthplace?*' 'Where were you *born?*' 'I was *born in Hamburg*' or even 'He *saw the light in Warsaw*'. It is clearly out of the question to draw up more or less complete lists of such exponents for all the notions listed in this study. Nor is it our aim to compose a phrase-book. Using language creatively is part of everyday speech, even at low levels of proficiency. At T-level a learner who has 'where' at his disposal (deixis: place), the verbal phrase 'to be born', the pronoun 'you' (deixis), and some basic grammatical rules, has the ability to inquire after a person's birthplace, even without having learnt the exponent 'where were you born?' by heart.

		names of the months P
		cardinal or ordinal numerals up to 31 P
		cardinal numerals used to indicate years, eg 1974 P
	birthday	birthday R
		When is your birthday?

1.5	*age*	
	age (= length of time a person has lived)	age R
		What's her age?
		I am ... (years old) P
		How old are you (is he, she, etc.)?
	old	old P
		I am too old for this
	young	young P
		This is a party for young people
	year	year P
		I am ... years old
	month	month P
		Our baby is six months old

1.6	*sex*	
	sex (= being male or female)	sex R
	male	man P
		boy P
		gentlemen (as on lavatory doors) R
		male R
		m P (writing only)
	female	woman P
		girl P
		ladies (as on lavatory doors) R
		female R
		f P (writing only)

1.7	*marital status*	
	married	married P
	single (= not married)	single R
		not married P
	family (= children)	family R
		children P
	husband	husband P
	wife	wife P
	child	child P

1.8	*nationality*	
	nationality	nationality R
		names of one's own nationality, of nationality of native speakers of the foreign language, of

111

		inhabitants of countries neighbouring one's own country P
		names of nationality of inhabitants of countries neighbouring the foreign-language country (countries) R
	foreign	foreign P
	foreigner	foreigner P
1.9	*origin*	
	place of origin	place of origin R
	country of origin	country of origin R
		Where are you (is he, she, etc) from? P
		I am from ... P
	port of embarkation	port of embarkation R
1.10	*profession, occupation*	
	occupation (= what one does for a living)	profession R
		occupation R
		job P
		what do you do (for a living)? R
		name of one's own occupation P
	factory	factory P
		I work in a factory
	labourer	labourer R
	office	office P
		I work in an office
	office-worker	office-worker R
		clerk R
		typist R
	farm	farm P
		I work on a farm
	farmer	farmer R
	business	business P
		I am in business
	business-man/woman	business-man/woman R
	shop	shop P
		I work in a shop
	shop-assistant	shop-assistant R
	baker	baker P
	butcher	butcher P
	grocer	grocer P
	greengrocer	greengrocer P
	to sell	to sell P
	to buy	to buy P
	hospital	hospital P
		I work in a hospital
	doctor	doctor P
		physician R
	nurse	nurse R
	school	school P

INTRODUCTION TO EXTRACTS III.2.a–d

From *Waystage* four extracts have been selected.

III.2.a gives the general introduction to the objective.
III.2.b deals with the principles used in 'deriving' this lower objective from Threshold Level.
III.2.c is the overall characterization of *Waystage*.
III.2.d is a sample from the content specification (language functions), which may be compared to the corresponding sample from the Threshold Level (extract III.1.g).

Extracts III.2.a–d   Extract III.2.a

from J A van Ek and L G Alexander, *Waystage/Waystage English*

1. General introduction

In 1975 the Council of Europe issued a document under the title of *The Threshold Level in a European unit/credit system for modern language learning by adults*. This was followed a year later by *The Threshold Level for modern-language learning in schools*.

The *Threshold Level* is an attempt to state as explicitly as possible what the learners will have to be able to do in a foreign language if they wish:

> 'to be able to cope, linguistically speaking, in temporary contacts with foreign language speakers in everyday situations, whether as visitors to the foreign country or with visitors to their own country, and to establish and maintain social contacts'.

In the European unit/credit system this objective is presented as the lowest level of general foreign language ability. It is assumed that the objective as defined represents the minimum that is required in order to function adequately in those communication situations in which the members of the target group, 'general beginners', are most likely to need the ability to use a foreign language. In the present state of our knowledge this can be no more than an assumption. It would appear, however, that this assumption is supported on a sufficiently large scale to justify its adoption as a working basis for the planning of modern language programmes. This means, in effect, that the Threshold Level is offered as the lowest terminal objective in these programmes and that the learners must be given every encouragement not to discontinue their studies before they have reached at least this objective. Yet, reaching the *Threshold Level* is by no means an undemanding task. With its emphasis on the ability to use the foreign language functionally in a large number of situations, with all the structural variety required for this and its vocabulary content of 1100–1500 items it will demand a sustained learning effort and at least some 120–200 hours of instruction. It is obvious that in the eyes of many learners – especially of those with little experience of educational success – such a learning task will look very formidable indeed.

Since it is the professed aim of the unit/credit scheme not only to provide opportunities for language learning but also to induce people to use these opportunities, it will be necessary to structure this learning task in such a way that it may be presented to the learner as a series of manageable steps rather than as one single daunting whole. Some sort of unit organization within the *Threshold Level* would therefore seem to be required. However, until more experience has been gained in the planning of *Threshold Level* courses, it would be premature to propose such a compartmentalization of the syllabus.

It was decided instead to begin by defining one intermediary objective, roughly halfway between zero and the *Threshold Level*. The definition of such an objective would serve at least two useful purposes. It would enable the designers to try out what they considered to be fundamental structuring principles, principles which might later on be applied in establishing a more ambitious unit structure. Secondly, it would provide an objective which many learners might be expected to be able to teach within a comparatively short period. It was felt that such a short-term objective, if given proper recognition, would be a powerful tool in promoting the motivation of particularly those learners who had not previously engaged in courses of longer duration. This objective was called *Waystage*. The term indicates that, within the unit/credit system, this objective is not presented as a terminal objective, but rather as an articulation point for courses leading up to *Threshold Level*. Learners whose successful completion of the first half of such courses is given due recognition will be encouraged, it is assumed, to undertake the additional learning effort which is needed to take them to full *Threshold Level*. In the system, the *Threshold Level* is presented as the lowest objective for general foreign language ability. *Waystage*, however, is not given the status of an objective 'in its own right'. It is presented as a possible objective for the first half of courses leading up to *Threshold Level*. Yet, we would fail in our attempt to make *Waystage* the powerful tool for increasing motivation it is meant to be if we relied on extrinsic motivation only. After studying for a year or even longer, many learners are hardly likely to be fully satisfied with just the teacher's approval, the acquisition of some 'credits' or a similar pat-on-the-back reward. Especially adult learners will need the intrinsic motivation of realizing that their learning efforts are successful in a more meaningful way in that their ability to cope with foreign language situations is significantly increasing. Consequently, even without being offered as a terminal objective, *Waystage* will have to constitute a worthwhile level of ability in that it will enable the learners to cope at least minimally in those communication situations which may be most directly relevant to them.

4. Waystage and Threshold Level

4.1 Principles of selection

Waystage is presented as an articulation point for courses leading up to *Threshold Level* (see Chapter 1). It follows from this that it will be aimed at the same target population (see 3.2) as the *Threshold Level*, taking into account the situations in which the members of the target population are most likely to need the ability to use the foreign language. It also follows that the content of *Waystage* must be selected from that of the *Threshold Level*.

What principles are to be applied in making this selection? The first principle is that the widest possible functional range should be achieved as early as possible. Even the most naive learners start a foreign language course with the expectation that it will enable them to *do* things in the foreign language, particularly to do those things which they feel they may want to do when in contact with foreign-language speakers. In order to sustain their motivation we shall consequently have to plan their foreign language course in such a way that they can do as many of these things as possible as early as possible. To give a simple example: rather than teaching them from the start to introduce themselves in three different ways, we would prefer them to be able to do three different things each in one way. The range of expression required for fully adequate foreign language behaviour will be reached gradually. In our example this means that we would come back to *'introducing onself'* at a later stage in order to teach the other two ways of doing it. This 'recycling' is, of course, not only a grading principle below *Threshold Level*, it applies equally above it.

The second principle of selection is the old principle of increasing complexity. The language forms chosen for the first stage will, on the whole, be the simpler ones. 'Perhaps he is ill' rather than 'He may be ill', to give one example.

The third principle is that of immediate relevance. We cannot teach everything at the same time, we cannot deal with all the topics simultaneously. A selection will therefore have to be made of those topics which are likely to appeal most directly to the learners, ie those topics which they probably feel they most urgently need to be able to talk about.

The fourth principle is that of pedagogical adequacy. The selection we make will have to form a good basis for further learning. This is to say that it will not be a list of phrase book expressions to be learned parrot-fashion but that it will have to reflect the systematic properties of the language. Although the grammar contained in it will necessarily be a very incomplete one, it will nevertheless constitute a coherent body of rules, which the learners will have to be able to use creatively in their own foreign-language behaviour.

2. Waystage: Characterization

1. At *Waystage* the learners will have completed the first stage of a two-stage learning process ultimately resulting in a basic general foreign language ability (*Threshold Level*).

2. At *Waystage* the learners will already have the ability to fulfil the most essential language functions in a simple way and to cope, linguistically speaking, in a restricted number of foreign-language situations, especially those in which the use of the foreign language is likely to be found essential for the satisfaction of the most urgent communication needs.

3. *Waystage*, like *Threshold Level*, is an objective for those learners who would be temporary visitors to a foreign-language country or have temporary contacts with foreign-language speakers in their own country, and who would use the foreign language particularly orally and for general, non-professional purposes.

4. Although *Waystage* is a basis for achieving general foreign language ability it particularly favours the following topic areas:

   1. Personal identification
   2. House and home
   3. Free time, entertainment
   4. Travel
   5. Health and welfare
   6. Shopping
   7. Food and drink
   8. Services
   9. Places
   10. Language
   11. Weather
   12. Public notices.

5. At *Waystage* the learners will be able to fulfil the following language functions:

1. Imparting and seeking factual information

1.1 identifying
1.2 reporting (including describing and narrating)
1.3 correcting
1.4 asking.

2. Expressing and finding out intellectual attitudes

2.1 expressing agreement and disagreement
2.2 denying something
2.3 expressing that one knows or does not know something or someone
2.4 inquiring whether someone knows or does not know something or someone
2.5 accepting an offer or invitation
2.6 declining an offer or invitation

2.7   expressing ability and inability
2.8   inquiring about ability and inability
2.9   expressing how certain or uncertain one is of something
2.10 expressing one is/is not obliged to do something
2.11 inquiring whether one is obliged to do something
2.12 seeking and giving permission to do something
2.13 stating that permission is withheld.

3. Expressing and finding out emotional attitudes

3.1   expressing pleasure, liking
3.2   expressing displeasure, dislike
3.3   inquiring about liking, dislike
3.4   expressing satisfaction
3.5   expressing dissatisfaction
3.6   expressing disappointment
3.7   expressing preference
3.8   expressing gratitude
3.9   expressing intention
3.10 inquiring about intention
3.11 expressing want, desire
3.12 inquiring about want, desire.

4. Expressing moral attitudes

4.1   apologizing
4.2   granting forgiveness
4.3   expressing approval
4.4   expressing appreciation
4.5   expressing regret
4.6   expressing indifference.

5. Getting things done (suasion)

5.1   requesting others to do something
5.2   warning others to take care or to refrain from doing something
5.3   instructing or directing others to do something
5.4   offering assistance
5.5   requesting assistance
5.6   making suggestions.

6. Socializing

6.1   greeting people
6.2   when meeting people
6.3   when introducing people and when being introduced
6.4   when taking leave
6.5   attracting attention
6.6   proposing a toast.

6. At *Waystage* the learners will be able to do at least the following things[11] with regard to each topic area:

1. Personal identification

Say who they are, spell their name, state their address, give their telephone number, say when and where they were born, state their age, sex, say whether they are married or not, state their nationality, say where they are from, what they do for a living, describe their family, state their religion, if any; obtain similar information from others.

2. House and home

Describe a house or flat and the room in it, refer to and inquire about furniture and bedclothes, services and amenities, describe regions, particularly the one where they themselves live.

3. Free time, entertainment

Say when they are free and what they do in their spare time, particularly with reference to public entertainment, sports, reading; obtain similar information from others.

4. Travel

Use means of public transport, obtain tickets, etc, refer to means of private transport, seek accommodation, book a room, inquire about meals, etc.

5. Health and welfare

Describe what is wrong to a doctor or a dentist, report accidents, say whether they feel well, are hungry, tired, etc, obtain articles of personal hygiene, refer to medical services and emergency services.

6. Shopping

Use shopping facilities, particularly obtaining foodstuffs, clothes and household articles, discuss prices, pay for things bought.

7. Food and drink

Refer to and order various kinds of food, also in a restaurant.

8. Services

Refer to and inquire about postal services, telephone, telegraph, bank and police.

---

[11] These 'behavioural specifications' are to be regarded as guidelines, rather than exhaustive descriptions. In fact, the possibilities of relating the ability specified under 'language functions' and 'general notions' to the various topic areas are so numerous that an exhaustive description, even at this level, would seem to be hardly feasible.

9. Places

Ask the way and give strangers directions.

10. Language

Say how well they speak, understand, read, write a foreign language, ask what things are called, what a word means, ask someone to speak slowly, to repeat something, ask whether something is correct, how something is pronounced.

11. Weather

Talk about various weather conditions.

12. Public notices

Understand the text of important signs.

Extract III.2.d

3. Waystage: Content specification[12]

The following abbreviations are used in the specifications:

NP : noun phrase, ie something which, in a sentence, has a nominal function;
VP : verb phrase, ie a verb or verbal group with objects, if any;
N : noun;
V_{inf} : infinitive without *to*;
V_{to} : infinitive with *to*.

Division I: Language functions with exponents for English

1. Imparting and seeking factual information

1.1	*identifying*	demonstrative pronouns *(this, that, these, those)* BE + NP (1) demonstrative adjectives *(this, that, these, those)* + N + BE + NP personal pronouns (subject forms) + BE + NP declarative sentences
1.2	*reporting (including describing and narrating*	What happened?
1.3	*correcting*	same exponents as above; in addition: adverb *no* negative sentences with *not* sentences containing the negation words *never, no* (adjective), *nothing*
1.4	*asking*	interrogative sentences (yes/no questions) question word sentences with *when, where, why, what* (pronoun), *who, what* (adjective), *how*, (+far, much, long, etc)

2. Expressing and finding out intellectual attitudes

2.1	*expressing agreement and disagreement*	Yes All right declarative sentences No (adverb) negative sentences with *not*
2.2	*denying something*	No (adverb) negative sentences with *not* sentences containing the negation words *never, no* (adjective), *nothing*

[12] Sample (Ed.).

121

2.3	*expressing that one knows or does not know something or someone*	I (don't) know (+noun (–group)/pronoun)
1.4	*inquiring whether someone knows or does not know something or someone*	Do you know (+noun (–group)/pronoun)
2.5	*accepting an offer or invitation*	Yes, please Thank you
2.6	*declining an offer or invitation*	No, thank you
2.7	*expressing ability and inability*	NP + can(not) + VP
2.8	*inquiring about ability or inability*	Can(not) + NP + VP
2.9	*expressing how certain/uncertain one is of something*	
	(a) positive	declarative sentences
	(b) intermediate	I think + (so (*that*–clause
	(c) weak	Perhaps . . .
	(d) negative	I don't think + (so (*that*–clause
2.10	*expressing one is/is not obliged to do something*	I (don't) have to + VP
2.11	*inquiring whether one is obliged to do something*	Do I have to + VP
2.12	*seeking and giving permission to do something*	May I/Can I + VP Yes All right
2.13	*stating that permission is withheld*	(Please) don't + VP No (adverb)

3. Expressing and finding out emotional attitudes

3.1	*expressing pleasure, liking*	This/that is (very) nice I like + noun (–group)/pronoun (very much)
3.2	*expressing displeasure, dislike*	He/she/this/that is not (very) nice I don't like + noun (–group)/pronoun
3.3	*inquiring about liking /dislike*	Do you like + noun (–group)/pronoun
3.4	*expressing satisfaction*	This/that is very good/nice

from J L M Trim in: *Modern Languages (1971–1981)*

PROGRESS TOWARDS A MORE COMPREHENSIVE FRAMEWORK FOR THE DEFINITION OF LANGUAGE-LEARNING OBJECTIVES

Whilst is is undoubtedly very largely the various Threshold Level specifications that have established the reputation of the Council of Europe Modern Languages Projects, it has been clear to the Project Group for some time that this form of specification does not exhaust the objectives which language learners should set themselves. Thus, S Salin reports a Swedish work group as saying: 'In Swedish curricula general, non-subject-specific goals are also usually incorporated. The group found it essential that such goals as personal and social development of the individual, capacity for co-operation and critical thinking, tolerance and understanding should be included in the curricula'.

Accordingly, the Project Group set up in 1979 a working party to consider 'an overall model for the specification of language-learning objectives more complex than those set out in the Threshold Level documents'.

The various Threshold Level documents are concerned with the learner as potential communicator and set out in detail the knowledge, skills and behaviour required of a language learner in order for him or her to be able to participate effectively in interpersonal communication in the situations of everyday life. As such, they represent an attempt, based on an intuitive needs analysis, to forsee the basic properties of the communication situations with which he may expect to be faced. This explicitness has enabled testers, course developers, teachers, parents and learners all to have a much clearer understanding of the uses to which they will be putting the language they learn. Learning has become more purposive and better motivated. Users have not had difficulty in adjusting the proffered specifications to the needs of the students actually before them.

However, terminal objectives, even when stated in clear operational terms, though necessary, are not sufficient for educational planning. They have to be situated in a more comprehensive framework of educational aims and objectives which are none the less important for being resistant to exact operational specification. In an educational context we are not simply concerned with training certain kinds of skilled behaviour, but also (especially when it comes to the education of young people at school, but also in adult education) with the steady and purposive development of the learner as a communicator and as a learner, as well as with his personal and social development. Preparing to be an effective communicator certainly means acquiring the knowledge of a linguistic system and the conditions of its use in order to realize one's communicative intentions in the situations of daily life. In many cases the Threshold Level documents specify the particular words, phrases and structures the use of which will express a particular communicative intent. It may appear that the ability of a learner to deal with the situations which confront him will be strictly

123

dependent on the extent to which the course planner or teacher has foreseen them. In fact, as van Ek has pointed out, this is true mainly of the topic-related specific notions, dealing generally with concrete features of the here and now. Speech act functions and general notions and their linguistic exponents are not bound to any one situational context. The learner who has acquired them can bring them to bear in a much wider range of situations which have not been foreseen, or when a particular situation takes an unpredictable turn. Indeed, it is one of our characteristics as human beings that we are generally, as Vignaux points out, not satisfied to conform to a set routine. We feel a drive to express ourselves as particular individual personalities in our exchanges with our fellows. The richness of experience in the 'Actes de parole' in Un niveau-seuil is at least partly intended to enable us to select what suits us as people of a particular character and temperament, and to recognize these features in other people's speech. Then the development of creativity in the learner is necessary as well as conformity to socially established norms. To find the proper balance between the two is one of the principal challenges to learners and teachers alike.

Another important aspect of learning to communicate not developed in the threshold level specifications is the development of conversational strategies. We give the learner ways of performing particular functions and expressing particular notions, but leave it to him as to how he should combine them into sensible discourse, as he works together with another speaker of the language to identify and tackle a common problem. As, say, in chess, to know the rules of the game and the different moves that can be made is no guarantee of being able to develop winning combinations. The need for the learner to handle chains of speech-acts has been recognized by the Council of Europe team from its earliest days (cf Trim, J L M (1973b) and Bung K (1973a).)

In educating a learner to become an effective communicator, our aim cannot be simply to provide him with ready-made responses to predictable situations, useful though these certainly are. In addition, it is part of our task to enable him to bring to bear an *always* inadequate equipment to cope with partly foreseen, partly unpredictable human interactions. As he does so, the inner resources he builds up form a more extensive and coherent system for communication than the simple addition of those pieces of language he has been explicitly taught or exposed to. On the basis of this experience he constructs, so far as possible, a model of the language being learnt. In addition to those (possibly innate) general principles which enable a child to construct a language model from limited exposure to experience, a second language learner has a very detailed model to assist him in the mother tongue and all its properties. One may say that a second language learner has only to acquire those features which are neither universal nor otherwise present in the mother tongue. Thus for a Dutch learner of German, subordinate clauses involve the learning of a set of words (subordinating conjunctions) and of course the skill of manipulating more, and more complex, conceptual material in a single linguistic operation. The English, or French, learner has in addition a complex of syntactic features to learn, which greatly increases the demands made upon him. A very high proportion of generalizations from particular experience in the light of an internalized model of the language being learnt are valid, appropriate, successful, and therefore unnoticed. Errors commonly result from:

a. the filtering effect of a pre-existing model (especially the mother tongue) on experience. We often do not perceive differences we have not been trained or alerted to perceive;

b. false generalizations based either on what we assume, wrongly, to be universal principles or on the particular patterning of the mother tongue. As with a growing child, these 'rules' characterize a converging series of 'interlanguages', which the individual constructs on his way to a stable, mature competence closely similar to that of other mature members of the language community (but never perhaps identical);

c. an overloading of the individual capacity to process thought into speech and vice versa, and

d. behavioural instability and memory lapses, producing slips of the tongue, false starts, wrong category assignments, etc. All speakers are subject to these, even in the mother tongue. In a second (foreign) language, which is far less established and consolidated, the instability is of course greater.

An understanding of these fundamentals profoundly affects our objectives and methods, both of teaching and evaluation, in guiding the language learner. Above all, once we realize that we can do no more than guide and influence a process of growth which necessarily involves experimentation, trial and error, much unnecessary purism falls away, as does the myth of the idealized native speaker. We are obliged to see communication as a process by which two (or more) individuals, each with a different experiential background, use speech on the basis of a partly shared, but always distinct, language model, to come to terms with each other and the requirements of a social situation involving them both. If we are to educate young people, or adults, to participate effectively in social co-operation and what J R Firth once called 'speech fellowship', we are as much concerned with the formation of attitudes and personality development as we are with the inculcation of knowledge and skills. It is of course much more difficult, if not impossible, to convert an aim of this kind into explicit behavioural objectives. Nevertheless, we need to monitor carefully the teaching methods and tests we employ in order to ensure that, in pursuing the operational objectives we can make explicit, we do not find that we are in fact blocking the proper development of the type of communicative personality we ought to be promoting.

It will be seen that the proper consideration of the learner as communicator necessarily brings in the understanding of the learner as a learner and as an individual personality. There are, however, further educational aims and objectives to be dealt with under these headings.

The development of the learner *qua* learner can be seen to be of considerable importance from the fact, revealed by the Brighton studies of the audience for successive BBC language courses, and by the Ealing study of needs analysis in polytechnics, that previous language learning experience is the most important single factor in determining whether a potential learner does in fact take up an offered language course in further and adult education. Since we know that the particular language studied by a pupil at school may well not be that for which a real need arises in adult life, one of the main benefits a child derives from school language studies may be the study skills and confidence in his ability to overcome obstacles to communication which enable him to meet the challenges which adult life may bring. Lack of experience and lack of confidence are undoubtedly one of the principal inhibitory factors which act as a bar to the full exploitation of the opportunities for mobility which already exist and will greatly increase over the next generation.

These inhibitions may be strongest among working populations who may have most to gain from mobility. A restricted but successful language-learning experience will not only give them confidence and some study skills. It should also make them aware of the validity of other modes of speech, thought and action, of the possibility of living with another people and another culture.

This liberation from a narrow-minded belief that only one's own language and culture are valid, others being comic, contemptible or threatening, leads to the last group of objectives which have formed the object of the group of studies aimed at producing a comprehensive framework for the statement of language-learning objectives – the development of the individual personality in both its cognitive and affective aspects.

Needs-based, learner-centred communicative language teaching is at a considerable remove from the grammar-translation method by which teachers, deriving their attitudes, aims, objectives and methods from the traditions of Classics, sought to train the minds of the young. Viewed as a formal system, a natural language displays an intimate mixture of the rational and the arbitrary, calling on the learner for considerable feats of memory, the rational application of general rules, alertness in watching for exceptions to those rules and a sensitivity to the fine shades of meaning which distinguish near-synonyms from one another. To take groups of pupils fairly fast through the increasing complexities of a language was seen as a good way of identifying an intellectual (and, through the associated study of great literature, a cultural) elite, prepared for the administration of various human institutions which all display the same half rational, half empirical character. The adherents of this view of modern languages (the very name 'modern' languages brings them into a single system with 'classical' languages) are still numerous and powerful, especially in higher education and the more prestigious schools. They view communication teaching as substituting banal and trivial pragmatism for the serious mental training of the past, with the abandonment of serious educational and cultural aims. Accordingly, they resist the intrusion of communicative objectives and methods into higher secondary and university studies. This 'classicial paradigm' is unlikely to be superseded until we can demonstrate that (a) the exploration in depth of human social interaction through language is an intellectually rewarding study, (b) the more closely controlled modes of expression and comprehension through written language are themselves ways of communicating, appropriate to some situations of human interaction and not to others, and (c) that an understanding of the cultural values and background which we presuppose in acts of communication is part of the communicative approach. Spoken and written modes, formal and informal styles, everyday life and other cultural manifestations, general and specialized usage, are all thus not to be presented as a series of either/or choices for an educational system, but assigned each its proper place in language education according to the needs, motivations, characteristics and resources of learners and society. In addition to cognitive development, affective development may be promoted by the enlargement of the young person's sympathies, replacing intolerance and fear of the unfamiliar by understanding and acceptance of the validity of other ways of living, and a more secure acceptance of one's own identity.

The following statement of aims, both those of a general educational character and those specific to language learning, may perhaps serve as a comprehensive general framework of objectives for language learning. It is, of course, a long step from establishing such a set of aims to putting them into practice in specific educational situations, but their acceptance on a European scale would at least mean that the profession would be pursuing, in different ways from place to place and time to time, a set of common goals. We can then see how best to co-ordinate our efforts.

The educational aims of modern language study
(adapted from the report of a working party of the British National Congress on Languages in Education on "Criteria for modern language examining at 16+")

1. General aims

The overall aim of the education of the individual is to promote his cognitive and affective development and to enable him to play a full part in the life of the community at work and at play as well as in exercizing the rights and duties of citizenship.

Cognitive (intellectual) development includes:

- learning both by enquiry processes and from exposition;
- storing and recognizing factual knowledge (including recognizing factual errors) and recalling factual knowledge in relevant situations;
- relating facts together to establish generalizations, hypotheses and theories;
- using data in illustrating or testing a statement, argument, assumption, hypothesis or conclusion;
- applying facts, principles, knowledge and skills in new situations;
- understanding and using the ways of thinking and modes of enquiry underlying a subject and the content to be learned;
- identifying and distinguishing fact, opinion, supporting or contradicting evidence, bias, assumption, proof, propaganda, fallacy;
- clarifying issues and exercizing judgment on the basis of clear criteria;
- developing adequate means of expression for intellectual attitudes and operations.

Affective (emotional and moral) development includes:

- understanding and gaining control over one's own feelings and their expression;
- understanding and accepting the feelings of other people; developing empathy;
- accepting people with different social and ethnic backgrounds, avoiding rigidity and stereotyping;
- developing positive attitudes towards experience;
- developing self-awareness, self-confidence, self-reliance and self-direction;
- developing a zest for living and the full attainment of human potential;

- understanding and accepting the disciplines involved in acting as an effective member of a social group (the co-operative principle);
- managing disagreement and conflict without violence, hostility and hatred;
- developing a stable system of ethical values;
- making value judgments on the basis of ethical criteria and being willing and able to act upon them;
- developing adequate means of expressing emotional and moral attitudes.

2. Specific aims of modern language learning

In addition to promoting in its daily practice the general educational aims outlined above, modern language study has the following more specific aims:

- to extend the learner's horizon of communication beyond that of his own linguistic community;
- to enable him to communicate in face-to-face situations with speakers of another language;
- to enable him to search for, discover and understand information relevant to his needs and interests through the medium of a foreign language;
- to enable him to realize the validity of other ways of organizing, categorizing and expressing experience, and of other ways of managing personal interactions;
- to raise his general level of language awareness, ie the characteristic properties and make-up of his own language in relation to those of another language, and of the uses to which language is put in everyday life;
- to develop his confidence, through a limited but successful experience of learning and using a foreign language, in his ability to meet the challenges posed by living in a foreign environment;
- to enable him to mediate between monolingual members of the two language communities concerned;
- to enable him imaginatively to extend the repertory of roles he can construct and play within contexts in which the foreign language can be used, such that he:

a.   engages purposively and appropriately in those contexts:
b.   reflects on the processes of language and of social interaction involved;
c.   develops his understanding of the complexities of personal interaction in social contexts;

- to enable him to develop the study skills necessary to the effective, self-directed study of other languages (or the same language to a higher level or for specific purposes) in later life;
- to give him (using language as a paradigm) insight into and experience of working within human institutions with their combination of partial systematicity and historically determined arbitrariness.

It should be emphasized that the more generalized aims and objectives listed here do not in any way replace or invalidate the Threshold Level definitions. They provide an overall framework within which detailed operationally-defined objectives can be situated and courses leading to them can be evaluated.

COUNCIL
OF EUROPE

CONSEIL
DE L' EUROPE

4 CHAPTER FOUR: 4

METHODOLOGY

INTRODUCTION TO CHAPTER FOUR

In the following extract Daniel Coste briefly reviews the methodological issues which have received special prominence in the various teaching/learning experiments aiming at the application of the principles evolved in the Modern Languages Project. These experiments are varied and heterogeneous. They do not form a coherent methodology. Although such concepts as 'the communicative approach' and 'the notional-functional approach' are closely associated with the work of the Project Group, it has never been the direct aim of the Group to set up a new 'Methodology'. Rather, the Group has sought to create the conditions which would allow new and effective methodological practices to be evolved and adopted. It has done so through the dissemination of a set of principles and a number of tools. Although this procedure predictably gave rise to a reconsideration of current methodological practice and the introduction of new concepts and new lines of action, it did not preempt any decisions which are more appropriately made in the (experimental) classroom than around a conference table. Meanwhile, a rich fund of experience is being accumulated, not only in actual teaching but also in the professional preparation of those who are responsible for this teaching. It will be a new task for a Council of Europe Project Group to evaluate this experience, systematize it and pass it on to the teaching profession.

Extract IV

from D Coste in: *Modern Languages (1971–1981)*

II Methodological options and current experiments

II.1. Thanks to the conceptual and analytical instruments it has generated, essentially pre-pedagogical in function, the Project has encouraged, propagated and affected a large number of innovatory educational schemes. Some of these experiments have occasioned reports which have been gathered together and are to be published by the Council of Europe. In addition, specific studies and reports have given accounts of projects involving schools or education for migrant workers. The resultant fund of hypothesis and achievement, though sizeable, accounts for only a fraction of work in and outside Europe referring back to the Modern Languages Project.

To sum up this variety of work here is out of the question. Each project is set in a specific context, and none sets out to discover some universally valid magic formula or to make hard-and-fast methodological prescriptions. But from this impressive crop, which testifies to the considerable impact of the Modern Languages Project, one can single out a few major trends and common characteristics.

II.2 Major trends

As is to be expected, when a set of hypotheses is advanced and a great many attempts are made to implement them, various trends emerge in the experimental here and now. At the risk of over-simplifying, inevitably standing back a little from the actual variables, we shall concentrate on four possible interpretations of these trends.

II.2.1 The importance of the threshold levels and the notional-functional approaches

The Modern Languages Project, it has been suggested, has often been made known in educational circles through specific studies: the threshold levels (notably *The Threshold Level* and *Un niveau-seuil*). These tools for constructing learning objectives have undoubtedly fulfilled their purpose by helping to redefine precisely the goals aimed at by given groups. But beyond this, the manner in which they are constructed has also been used ever more widely in curriculum and course design. This has taken on various forms, whose common denominator is emphasis on the identification and organization of teaching syllabuses.

In most cases, the indebtedness is first and foremost to the division into functions and notions, together with minor adjustment and adaptation. Syllabuses and courses then allow of detailed 'inventorial' descriptions: teaching items and aims are systematically classifiable with the help of the threshold levels categories (left-hand column) and exemplifications (right-hand column). It is obvious what makes the notional-functional inventories a convenient substitute for the lexical and grammatical inventories which formed the corpus and determined the division into teaching items in audio-lingual courses for instance. But it is equally obvious that this substitution

131

presents two main risks: (a) fragmentation of knowledge and capability without enough link-up between them; (b) maintenance of teaching practices whose stock-in-trade consists of repetitive, tedious, isolated exercises. These are risks, not foregone conclusions. But the fact remains that an obsession with endless lists often leads, in education as elsewhere, to a compartmentalization of tasks.

Sometimes the starting point is different, though often also based on proposals contained in the threshold levels: there is an attempt at a much broader characterization of the communicative situations the learner wants to master in the foreign language, and even though notions and functions are brought in at the next or next-but-one stage to refine the analysis of aims, it by no means follows that they become the basis of course planning, influencing the type of exercise recommended, for example. What tends to happen is that simulation exercises are suggested to the learner, who is asked to interpret, reproduce or produce exchanges in a given set of circumstances (ie in which the interlocutors' intentions and status, the aim of the exchange etc are specified).

With both of these options, one problem those responsible for experiments have usually wanted to raise has been what type of progression to adopt, ie primarily how to group together and sequence the study units. Regardless of the chosen criteria – linear, spiral, predominantly linguistic or otherwise – there is also anxiety about the relationship between functions, notions and situations, and the grammatical organization of the natural language in question: surely fragmentation or indiscriminately lumping things together lead to poor, haphazard or (from the learner's point of view) uneconomical presentation of grammar functions? But whatever else is expected from communication-orientated teaching, no one would dream of considering that there had been no acquisition of a linguistic competence. Suffice it to say that across the extremely wide range of pedagogical experiments referring back to the Threshold Levels, one of the recurrent concerns is with the place of grammar, and how to link up the pragmatic and linguistic aspects in a course using what is often nowadays termed the 'communicative approach'. Here there has been notable work by J Courtillon suggesting connections for French between language forms and communicative practices, in the interests of planned progression.

II.2.2 Learner-centred teaching and learner autonomy

Making the learner central to the didactic enterprise is not just a case of paying attention at the planning stage, in the choice of materials, procedures and exercises, to what he is and what his aims are. It can also involve the much more radical proposition that it is for the learner to organize and direct his own learning, taking genuine responsibility for decisions about aims, content, means and assessment. Experiments with adult learners at the CRAPEL, Nancy, go very definitely in this second direction, and it is clear in such cases that the connection with the principles of the Modern Languages Project is more a case of building on previous knowledge and on the learner's own strategies, of respecting and developing his autonomy, than of using tools such as the threshold levels to devise instructional sequences.

Simply because of its more resolutely innovatory character, this second trend will no doubt be regarded as less immediately usable, less charted than the former. We shall simply make three points.

1. The sort of initiative learners are allowed will naturally vary a lot depending on their educational history (or lack of it), and on their personal working style and working habits. They are equally at liberty to try out new procedures, vary materials and treatment or stick to some traditional exercise with which they have long been familiar.
2. Organizers of experiments of this sort readily acknowledge the need to combine self-directed learning with learning to be autonomous: for the learner to display autonomy, you must first (or simultaneously) teach him how; otherwise you are in danger of only giving to those who have, and using types of education which, in sociological terms, primarily benefit those who – with more (and more varied) educational experience behind them – are best able to manage their own learning effectively anyway.
3. Learning to be autonomous and self-directed learning do not mean that teachers take a back seat and resign: instead we see a proliferation and diversification of teachers' roles (teacher, technician, adviser, resource person, organizer, arbiter, etc), the need for which is soon apparent, just as a proliferation and diversification of teaching materials and types of learning activity are vital to give learners yet another opportunity to choose, try out procedures and revise or alter their own strategies.

II.2.3 Genuine tasks and instrumental use of the language
in the actual learning process

A third potential polarity in current experiments consists in looking, above all during the learning activity itself, for everything requiring the use of the language as an instrument for communication and action. The aim is not so much to 'simulate' exchanges which would be 'authentic' outside the classroom, or to 're-create' in the teaching context 'situations' which the foreign-language learner can reasonably expect to have to cope with once he has finished the course. The object is, as far as possible, to develop instrumental uses of the language being learned as part of the actual learning process: there may be an attempt to offer technical, artistic or games-playing activities which are intrinsically interesting, useful or enjoyable (a group game, preparing a recipe, constructing something, etc) and activate language for some practical purpose which is worthwhile in itself and not an obvious pretext, a necessary pretence at simulated communication; or there may be recourse to various forms and degrees of immersion, eg using the foreign language to teach new disciplines, knowledge or skills which are important, say, at school, whether in geography, physics or sport.

Note that in both cases the tasks performed are describable, down to their linguistic components, with the help of the notional-functional categories suggested by the Modern Languages Project for the construction of objectives (which does not of course mean that these categories exhaust the scope for description). A particular game may require an oral description of an object in terms of size, shape, texture, colour, etc; using a particular piece of apparatus may require the reading of instructions (imperatives, location in time and space). A given physics lesson will presuppose the ability to take notes on cause and effect, or on a comparison of two experimental procedures, and so on. But although speech acts, general notions and specific notions can clearly serve to describe certain aspects of tasks as they are performed, and although the teacher is free, up to a certain point, to decide what notions and functions a given task will require or call into play, the fact remains that the choice of teaching methodology favours pragmatic macro-units and not, to begin with, the notional-functional breakdown.

II.2.4 Combined and multi-media approaches

A fourth identifiable trend is one that borrows in various proportions from the three we have just tried to single out; its aim is, as it were, not so much their fusion into a homogeneous course (an undertaking which is doomed to failure), as bringing them together within a single educational aim and in a single set of learning materials.

A multi-media approach seems likely to permit this proximity (more a case of optional complementarity than of latent conflict or wilful confusion) between:

a.   teaching proposals emphasizing (cf II.2.1) a gradual, ordered progression (with a notional/functional and/or linguistic and/or situational bias, it being clearly understood that in this working method these various dimensions are in any case to be explicitly linked together;

b.   a major hypothesis preserving and developing learner autonomy, while allowing the learner as large an element of initiative and choice as possible (cf II.2.2) and giving him the use of an extensive battery of tools for his learning scheme;

c.   a range of tasks in which the foreign language sustains or assists the performance of operations which are not simply a matter of producing/interpreting language and which present an interest other than a purely language-learning one (cf II.2.3).

To suggest that a multi-media approach seems well suited to this type of 'marriage' does not, of course, mean that all multi-media courses fit this conceptual frame. But it is a reasonable assumption that the potential applications of each medium (television, radio, the printed word, cassettes, etc), together with the scope resulting from combinations of them, ought to make it easier to devise an educational project in line with the composite trend broadly outlined here, but of which a clearer picture emerges in various field projects.

II.2.5 Observation

The trends singled out in the preceding paragraphs are a convenient way of categorizing current experiments explicitly or implicitly linked to the Modern Language Project's key ideas. The field is seemingly vast and takes in the main areas of innovation in modern language teaching/learning.

The very diversity of the schemes in Europe and beyond which refer to or exploit the Project's major orientations and its work demonstrates that the Project would be seriously diminished as regards its pedagogical implications if it were to be equated merely with the construction (albeit important) of notional-functional language teaching programmes. Just as it would be misleading and wrong to claim that the variety of the new experiments comes directly or exclusively from what has been achieved within the Council of Europe, so also it would be going to the opposite extreme and a strangely blinkered approach to make out that the main impact of the Strasbourg proposals is primarily apparent in the debate about the selection and ordering of teaching syllabuses.

If this were really so, it would be hard to see the full significance ascribed to 'learning to communicate' in the first lines of this section of the report squaring with the effects and facts. But more of this later.

II.3 Common features

The four simple and compound trends just distinguished present, it seems to us, a number of common features, sometimes more pronounced, sometimes less so, but which surface fairly consistently. Insofar as these features – without in the least involving any one single methodology – to our mind break with what were, not so long ago, established practices and principles, they need listing, however briefly. There are five which concretely affect the learning situation: plurality, juxtaposition, explicitation, negotiation and evaluation. The important point, apart from the fact that each of them exists, is that they go together and combine.

II.3.1 Plurality

For our purposes, plurality means the diversity of materials and practices henceforth regarded as usable with learners and calculated to assist learning: authentic and fabricated texts, aids of various kinds, conventional exercises (including the famous fill-in exercise, dictation and memorization of verb tables) and exercises of a more innovatory turn (role-playing, problem-solving, selective comprehension of written or recorded material, etc . . .); nothing is ruled out *a priori*, even by the trends which place more emphasis on communication situations and communicative tasks.

II.3.2 Juxtaposition

Juxtaposition occurs where the above plurality is not necessarily accompanied by a determination to incorporate a range of materials and practices into an overall scheme in which each component has its allotted place and function in a single, supposedly watertight methodological hypothesis (whatever that hypothesis may be). The usual layout chosen implies on the whole that, since learning paths and strategies can be varied to suit different learners, or one and the same learner, and since the proposals in the pedagogic armoury must offer inbuilt scope for choice, adjustment and changes of emphasis, the only acceptable solution is to juxtapose the different materials and procedures – which neither means a complete hotch-potch nor heralds the triumph of a weary 'anything goes' approach using whatever comes to hand on the pretext that 'we don't know how it works anyway'. It is just that the co-existence of a number of partial local coherencies is considered workable, and it is felt to be the learner himself who, in the course of his own learning, out of these partial coherencies (the coherency of a task or series of tasks, the coherency of a notional-functional classification, the coherency of a grammatical description, the coherency of a role or combination of roles, etc) constructs the more or less transient systems of his communicative competence in the foreign language.

II.3.3 Explicitation

In most teaching experiments, plurality and juxtaposition, as defined, will necessitate frequent resort to explicitation. It is no longer possible to teach by implication alone, as do methods which deliberately refrain from grammatical commentary, background information or explaining the why and wherefore of a given teaching technique, concentrating exclusively on practising production/decoding of utterances. Of course, whether the methodologists like it or not, 'meta'-discourse, talking about language, culture and education, is never totally absent from the didactic process, but the point here is that plurality and juxtaposition mean that teachers and learners must resort to it more often, and where explicitation about available materials, procedures, decisions, strategies, becomes, if not totally unavoidable, at least 'usual' and frequently expected, whether it involves explaining to others or to oneself an operation, a norm, or aspects of a choice or decision. This new functional importance of explicitation and its incorporation into the very dynamic of the educational project presupposes the existence and perfection of suitable instruments, as well as requiring that the learner possess, or gradually procure, the means – linguistic means, especially – to participate fully in this area as well.

II.3.4 Negotiation

The point needs no labouring, but the common features mentioned make it well-nigh essential (especially in any teaching operation where the class or group lend their collective dimension to the teaching/learning process) to set up negotiating structures, rules and arrangements. The way education is managed is no longer obvious, or necessarily in keeping with the time-honoured patterns of the school-masterly tradition; it therefore requires the offering of explanations and the adoption of revisable – as it were, contractual – agreements within the class or group of learners. As with explicitation, to which it is obviously akin, negotiation must no longer be rather marginal, a case of peripheral concessions to the pupils' wishes or the passing vogue, but an important, and indeed key aspect of course planning. Here, too, acquiring and using the means to negotiate (notably, but not exclusively, language ones) will doubtless be a frequent priority though the means are of course useless on their own, being meaningful only in relation to bargaining points and structures.

II.3.5 Assessment

One of the things requiring negotiation (and preliminary explanation) is assessment. Obviously, without the possibility of gauging where individuals stand and what progress they are making within the complex scheme resulting from the foregoing, any number of things can go wrong and keeping a check will be difficult. In addition to its conventional and basic function of measuring the changes which occur in the course of education, assessment clearly acts as a regulator of the total teaching operation. This role is admittedly also conventional, like it or not: assessment, by examination and certification of course, is not just a means of measuring results and awarding marks; it also exerts a considerable influence on syllabus content and classroom practice. The phenomenon is a familiar one, even though it is one of those obligations to which education sometimes turns a blind eye. But we have something else in mind, something which is indicative of the interrelatedness (if not interdependence) of the common features listed: in educational experiments which, underneath assorted trends, seemingly point to the regular occurrence and gradual spread in actual teaching practice of what we have termed plurality, juxtaposition, explicitation and negotiation, assessment clearly looks to be the teachers' and learners' sole means of knowing when to adjust, change or correct given aspects of the individual's or the group's work, insofar as this assessment, along the lines indicated, is itself plural, explicitated and negotiated. There is still a lot to do before we can go further in this direction: this is one of the basic prerequisites for any systemic approach to classroom situations, but it is here also – unsurprisingly – that the greatest obstacles remain (which are not all institutional ones, being linked, too, to the way most teachers and most learners see the function, content and procedures of assessment).

II.3.6 Observation

Just as the major trends mentioned above testified that the pedagogical impact of the Modern Languages Project is not confined or solely due to the possible relations between notional-functional analysis and the construction of a teaching sequence, so that the common features just examined highlight the ways in which the introductory points about 'learning to communicate', as understood by the Modern Languages Project, are liable to impinge concretely on teaching/learning situations.

Explicitation and negotiation presuppose that the learners are regarded from the outset, possibly as 'foreign-language beginners', but most definitely as fully-fledged communicators. The act of learning itself is a communication situated in space and time, and primarily a communication linked to the management of this act of learning.

There is every likelihood that teaching arrangements exhibiting the features considered will teach something else as well as forms of foreign-language communi- cation: the communicator-learner is changed by the very process in which he features as learner-communicator. Progress in autonomy and familiarization with self- assessment procedures for instance, but also involvement as a responsible agent in the social milieu and collective process in which the education takes place, are aspects of learning which cannot be reduced to the acquisition of knowledge and know-how in the foreign language, but affect the individual being educated in his entirety.

COUNCIL
OF EUROPE

CONSEIL
DE L' EUROPE

5 CHAPTER FIVE: 5
AUTONOMOUS LEARNING

INTRODUCTION TO CHAPTER FIVE

The desirability of promoting learner autonomy has already been mentioned in several earlier extracts. Indeed, the promotion of learner autonomy is an intrinsic element of learner-centred learning systems. Yet actual techniques for promoting this autonomy are still in their infancy. The most comprehensive study available is probably Henri Holec's *Autonomy and foreign language learning*, from which the following extract has been taken. Rather than offering ready-made solutions, it analyses the concept of learner autonomy. In the editors' view this is the essential first step towards developing the required techniques.

Extract V

from H Holec, *Autonomy and foreign language learning*

II. AUTONOMY AND SELF-DIRECTED LEARNING OF LANGUAGES

A simple way of describing the ability to take charge of language learning is to describe the practical modalities of decision-making which such ability renders possible.

Let us remind ourselves that, with total self-direction, action by the learner is concerned with:

— fixing the objectives
— defining the contents and progressions
— selecting the methods and techniques to be used
— monitoring the acquisition procedure
— evaluating what has been acquired.

Note: We are keeping this subdivision of the learning process but this does not mean that decisions at each of these levels can be made independently of decisions concerning the rest:

". . . components (of the education system) such as analysis of needs and evaluation of results must all be considered together and uninterruptedly throughout the entire process".[1]

1. Fixing of objectives

1.1.   Traditionally, ie in directed learning:

1.1.1.   The learning objectives are fixed by the teaching establishment or the teacher.

1.1.2.   This is done:

—through an analysis of the field in which the learning takes place: analysis of the linguistic code in the case of teaching linguistic competence and of verbal communication in the case of teaching communicative competence;

—through an 'objective' analysis of the civilization (in the broad sense) of the country of the target language, when the learning objective includes a 'cultural' dimension;

—lastly, if account is taken of the audience, through the learner's needs and motivations.

1.1.3.   The teaching establishment and teacher define these objectives on the basis of what they regard as the knowledge indispensable to the learner, taking the native speaker as a standard.

---

[1] Janne, H. (1977) Organization, content and methods of adult education. Report CCC/EES (77) 3, p. 23.

141

1.1.4. The objectives so determined:
— are fixed once and for all in the temporal framework of the learning (for a year, term, intensive session, etc);
— apply to all learners, usually a group;
— are, where necessary, subdivided into intermediate objectives so as to fit in with the teaching structure (objectives for each year in the case of a syllabus covering more than a year) or to conform to the learners' standards on admission, or else for both these reasons; we thus arrive at the 'pilgrim's progress' described by John Trim, adviser to the Modern Languages Project of the Council for Cultural Cooperation.[2]

1.2. In self-directed learning the learner himself defines his objectives and the essential consequence of this will be the introduction of the learner's *specific personal dimension*.[3]

1.2.1. Definition of the objectives will be based on an analysis made by the learner of the final behaviour aimed at, in accordance with his *subjective* criteria.

1.2.1.1.a As regards the communicative competence[4] the learner will take as objective not the verbal behaviour of the abstraction called 'native speaker' but that which he conceives as being his own in the communicative situations in which he will find himself. This will then be integrated behaviour (ie dissociated neither from the situation nor, above all, from the learner himself) described, for example, with the help of statements of the type:
— "I must be capable of doing this in conversation with such and such a speaker, in such and such a sphere . . ."
— "If the person I am speaking to does this I must be capable of reacting in such and such a way . . ."

— "I must be capable of doing (a) and (b) in such and such a manner (cordial/reserved, amusing/serious, formal/informal, quickly/speed being of no consequence, my pronunciation must be perfect/my pronunciation will be of no consequence so long as I am understood, and so on)."

It is thus not only at the level of the *choice* of the communicative acts that the individual character of the learning will appear but also (and it is essentially here that the definition of objectives will show the greatest difference from determination by the teacher or teaching establishment) at the level of the *ways* in which the acts are realized: for a learner who envisages himself as a future speaker the dimensions 'attitude towards the other person', 'personal involvement', 'image of oneself', etc, all of them expressed by verbal behaviour, are naturally an integral part of communication. That which objectively viewed may be considered as a 'variant' may for the learner be the personal norm that he desires to reach :[5] it is in effect (the equivalent as

---

[2] *cf* Trim, J L M (1980) *Developing a unit/credit scheme of adult language learning* Pergamon, Oxford.

[3] In order to make the statement clear and simple the remarks we shall suggest will be *generalizations:* they will be valid for the general body of learners without necessarily being so for each individual one.

[4] An adult is never interested in linguistic competence alone.

[5] In this sense an analysis of the needs on which the learner bases the fixing of his learning objectives brings into play a number of parameters not included in the analyses of 'external' needs which could moreover be included only after preparing a personality description scale.

regards communication) language-behaviour which he wishes to make his own, an 'idiolect', and not a language-system.

1.2.1.1.b   On the other hand, as regards the attainment threshold laid down by the learner for each of his objectives, the personal dimension will once again play its part: he himself will decide what is indispensable, what is secondary and what is useless. As a result the attainment threshold aimed at will vary according to the learner's 'temperament' and there will be a wide gap between the threshold of the 'perfectionist' and that of the 'laxist'.[6]

1.2.1.2.   In the same way as regards the cultural dimension of his learning only some aspects of the foreign civilization will be of real interest to him, namely those that will enable him to build up his own view of the civilization in question.

1.2.2.   The objectives and learning thresholds will not necessarily be fixed for all time; the learner may look at them again as his learning continues and alter them.

Any possible alterations, whether partial or total, may be the result of various factors.

1.2.2.1.   *Changes occurring in the external situation forming the learning environment:*

— professional or vocational situation: where the motive for learning is professional or vocational, any change in language needs connected with such occupation will involve a change of objective (eg a change in the function of communication in a foreign language as part of the work contemplated or a change in the work as a whole, and so on);
— social situation: where the motive for learning is a social one, certain changes in this field may involve a change of objective (eg where the learner wishes to be able to communicate among a circle of acquaintances, the addition of new individuals speaking a different dialect, etc);
— material situation: changes of all kinds may involve a change of objective (eg a move to another area making it possible to receive foreign television, etc).

1.2.2.2.   *Changes occurring in the internal learning situation:*

— level of knowledge: as his level of knowledge of the language he is learning changes the learner may be led to amend his initial objectives either because some objectives regarded as unattainable become attainable or on the other hand because objectives regarded as attainable prove unattainable or because fresh objectives are revealed in the light of knowledge already acquired; thus in fact developments in any learning experience may be the reason for a change in objectives;
— finally it must not be forgotten that the learner may simply change his mind.

---

[6] A learner fixing his threshold at a level which would not allow him to communicate (a currently widespread fear among language teachers) would simply reveal:
— either that he has not known how to make a proper evaluation (cf II–5: Evaluation) if he makes his assessment at the end of the course: or
— that mastery of a communicative competency is not his main purpose.

1.3.1.   As regards the definition of objectives therefore, self-direction of learning entails some very big differences as compared with definition made from outside by a teacher or teaching establishment. To sum up, the 'pilgrim's progress' towards an objective based essentially on the field of learning, the same for everyone, is replaced by progressive steps (a succession of objectives) of a diverse nature fixed for and by each learner by reference to his personal needs and motivations, progressive steps which may be challenged and amended by the learner at any time.

1.3.2.   To be autonomous is to be capable of dealing with the definition of objectives of this kind.

2.   Definition of the contents and progressions

The contents and progressions form the materials—and their sequential organization — which enable the objectives to be realized. Definition of them is closely linked with the definition of objectives and, indeed, it sometimes happens that one of them is defined in terms of the other.

2.1.   In directed learning the contents and progressions are defined by the teachers who 'have the knowledge'.

2.1.1.   The contents are defined in terms of lexis, grammar and phonology:
— as regards lexis the choice is usually made on the basis of frequency lists, possibly supplemented by a 'specialized vocabulary';
— as regards grammar the principle is approximately the same: basic structures and possibly distinct structures (stylistic dimension);
— as regards phonology, since the elements available for selection are somewhat limited in number the whole is generally made an integral part of the curriculum: pronunciation of phonemes, intonation, rhythm.

For all three components a single norm (dialect, register, level) is adopted, perhaps with a few limited incursions into other norms.

2.1.2.   In a general way the approach is 'globalistic', ie the contents are regarded as necessary for the learning of both comprehension and expression, sometimes even for both oral and written learning (this is essentially owing to the fact that methods of learning different skills are not generally differentiated one from another).

2.1.3.   With regard to progressions, these are based on the degree of 'profitability' of the elements incorporated as judged by frequency and on the degree of their complexity. The progressions are generally rather slow and result in learning being spread out over a rather long period.

2.2.   In self-directed learning the contents will as a general rule be defined by the learner, both in a more restrictive manner, to the extent that only those

---

[7] This section devoted to objectives should be closely related to that covering evaluation, since the objectives must be determined so as to be capable of evaluation, and since evaluation cannot be done except in relation to objectives. Some of the problems that may arise in this section will therefore find answers in the chapter on evaluation.

verbal elements necessary for realizing the selected communicative functions (cf objectives) are incorporated into the curriculum, and more widely, to the extent that mastery of the personal dimension of communication will require a number of additional verbal and non-verbal elements.

2.2.1.   One of the two fundamental features of definition of contents by the learner is that the thematic content of the communication aimed at is given priority. The learner wants above all to communicate (to understand and to express) significations and the choice of forms is made only secondarily by reference to significations. Thus the contents will be defined only secondarily in terms of lexis, grammar and phonology. The process will actually be as follows (expressed in terms of propositions which the learner will possibly be called upon to construct):

— which are the 'ideas' I wish to understand and which are the 'ideas' I wish to express?[8]
— which are the words and grammar I must master so as to understand the first and express the second?

As regards the choice of norm, this will be made in a much more flexible and more appropriate manner: it will be made on the basis of communicative situations (defined particularly by reference to the others involved in the conversations and the thematic content) and on the proposed method of communication (comprehension and/or expression).

Note: The thematic contents are of course determined on the basis of personal choices and not on the basis of the choices of the majority of the class-group or the subjective choices of the teacher.

2.2.2.   The second fundamental feature of the definition of contents by the learner is that those contents are no longer 'brought in' from outside but are to some extent 'created' by the learner. He will have to discover those contents by observing and analysing the sources of information available to him:[9] written texts, sound recordings, video recordings, films, dictionaries, grammars, etc. These sources will also include both educational and authentic documents, and native speakers.[10]

2.2.3.   As for progressions, these are determined not by reference to the linguistic content but on the basis of communicative and thematic priorities fixed by the learner for himself. As a rule they will be fairly rapid, since an adult learner is hardly ever in a position to spread his learning over a very long period of time.

---

[8] The two sets of 'ideas' may overlap, but not necessarily so (I may want to understand what my doctor tells me but the things I have to tell him may be quite different).

[9] Every discovery is a creation for the person making it even if the thing discovered was already known to others.

[10] Experience shows that this discovery is simpler than would appear since the learner has at his disposal the valuable tool consisting of the communicative and linguistic intuition acquired in his mother tongue. Moreover it becomes easier and easier as his knowledge increases.

2.3. Conclusions

2.3.1.   With regard to the definition of contents, the fundamental originality of acting on an autonomous basis is to be found firstly in the new way of looking at the knowledge to be acquired as presupposed by such definition and secondly in the new learner/knowledge relationship brought into operation (this will be referred to again in Chapter III, *cf* p 25 *et seq*). This means dividing knowledge into *useful knowledge* and *useless knowledge* at each stage of the learning, in a different manner from the 'traditional' division.

2.3.2.   With respect to definition of progressions, acting on an autonomous basis involves abandoning rigid progressions determined by reference to linguistic inventories prepared in a 'scientific' way, since immediate 'profitability' is more important than long-term 'profitability'.

2.3.3.   Being autonomous means being capable of defining the contents and progressions of one's learning in this way.

3.   Selection of methods and techniques

3.1.   Without going back to the various ways in which the choice of methods and techniques is carried out in self-directed learning, we may simply remind ourselves that the selection varies according to the greater or lesser amount of trust placed in one theory of learning or another, to the belief (sometimes amounting to fanaticism) in this or that teaching method, to the importance attached to one technical tool or another, but also according to the lessons drawn from experience, to the educational intuition gained by practice in combination with creative imagination, and so on and so on.

In the present state of knowledge regarding the process of language learning by adults it is a difficult and risky business to work out teaching methods and techniques suitable for the learners and this explains the great diversity of solutions suggested.[11]

3.2.   In self-directed learning the learner himself will be defining his methods and techniques.

3.2.1.   He will not make this definition *a priori* before starting his studies but right at the beginning and as his studies continue. He will in fact proceed by trial and error: by using the methods and techniques he has chosen and then evaluating them he will be able to decide which are appropriate to his own case.

3.2.2.   As a rule this empirical process will not involve any loss of learning time: in the first place the investment thus decided upon at the start of his studies will be to a large extent offset by the improved quality of later learning, besides this the number of trials and errors will never be very great since there is nothing to prevent the learner from thinking the matter over and picking out from all the possible alternatives those that are most likely to be suitable.

[11] The study of this process is only in its infancy *cf* the work done at Kiel University in the Federal Republic of Germany by Wode *et al*, and by Krashen *et al* at the University of Southern California, USA (*see Second language acquisition and second language learning* by Stephen Krashen (1981) Pergamon, Oxford).

3.2.3.   The methods and techniques that will be available to the learner include:

— those that he knows because he has used them in earlier studies (especially language studies);

— those he will learn of from other learners or in miscellaneous teaching materials;

— those he will devise for himself.

3.2.4.   The criteria he will use for selection purposes will be of two kinds:

— criteria of efficacy as regards the objectives set: knowing exactly what his objectives are and making his own assessments of progress made, the learner will be able to determine accurately enough how far the methods and techniques he has used have been effective; this judgment, coupled with what he has learnt during his studies, will enable him to make valid assumptions as to the reasons for the failure of any particular method or technique where he has been let down in any way and to plan his decisions for the next attempt;

— criteria regarding adaptation to external and internal constraints on the learner: the proposed methods and techniques must be adapted as far as possible to constraints of all kinds affecting the learner during his studies — restrictions in the matter of place, time, materials, etc — and must fit in as far as possible with the type of learner that every adult is — restrictions whose characteristics range from his type of memory to qualities such as perseverance, patience, and so on, and to the value attached by the learner to any particular activity.

3.3.   Conclusions

3.3.1.   Definition by the learner himself of the methods and techniques to be used in his studies is far more likely, in the present state of knowledge, to lead to success than is definition of them from outside. In a general way this is what happens when the 'consumer' is also the 'producer'. There is no doubt, however, that if, in the future, research into the acquisition of second languages could make it possible to enlighten and direct the learner's intuition, those chances would be enhanced still further.

3.3.2.   Being autonomous means being capable of selecting one's learning methods and techniques in the way we have just described.

4.   Monitoring the acquisition procedure

4.1   The acquisition procedure has reference to spatial and temporal dimensions: where the acquisition takes place, at what times, according to what timetable, at what rhythm, and so on. Adult audiences are distinctive in that contrary to 'vocational' learners involved in a schools system they are subject to spatial and temporal restrictions that are often very rigid and always very specific to each individual. Among those restrictions it should be in particular noted that very often the end of the course is fixed so far as the learner is concerned, either because he has been 'credited' a certain

147

length of time or because he has to make use of the ability he seeks to acquire at some definite time, determined in advance.

In these circumstances the learning rhythms are all the more varied because the speed of learning, which differs from one learner to another, is complicated by the multiplicity of overall timetables.

In addition the psychological and intellectual availability of adults with their professional and vocational commitments, together with fatigue and preoccupations of all kinds, is extremely irregular and unpredictable: the best time for learning and the length of time devoted to it occur at very different periods in time for different individuals.

4.2.   It is partly in order to cope with this situation that instruction tends towards individualization: distance teaching and programmed instruction, for example, must enable the learner to cope with the spatial and temporal restrictions imposed upon him by his environment and to arrange to do his learning at times most convenient to himself.

However, this is not always possible, especially where the course begins and ends for everyone at the same time, where the mid-term and final examinations are held on the same dates for everyone, and so on.

4.3.   In self-directed learning the student decides for himself when to study, how long to work at a time, and he can therefore adjust his learning rhythm to his acquisition rhythm. Where the end of the course is decided for him by others, he can to some extent overcome this restriction by speeding up his learning rhythm either by devoting more time to his studies or by increasing the number of maximally effective sessions.

5.   Evaluation of what has been acquired

'Evaluation of what has been acquired' may be understood to mean very different operations which need to be distinguished one from another.

5.1.   To begin with *evaluation* must be distinguished from *certification*.

"Evaluation functions and techniques should not be confused with those relating to certification . . . Certification necessitates evaluation, although the converse is not true".[12]

Certification is based on an appraisement of knowledge made by reference to and in order to obtain a certificate. It is an appraisement made outside the learning process and which obeys rules of a sociological nature in relation to which the learner as such has no power to make decisions. The only freedom allowed him is that of choosing whether or not he shall direct his learning towards obtaining a certificate.

In a self-directed system of learning the learner **must** be able to make a choice, which means that certification must not be compulsory:

"Certification should be confined to courses conferring qualifications: it should not be allowed to become the compulsory objective or the required terminus".[13]

[12] Porcher, L (1979) 'The functions of evaluation in a European unit/credit system for modern language learning by adults' in the *Report of the Symposium held at Ludwigshafen-am-Rhein, 7–14 September 1977.* Strasbourg.

[13] Schwartz, B (1977) *Permanent Education. Final report* CCC/EP (77) 8 revised.

5.2.   In evaluation, strictly speaking a distinction must be made between *external evaluation* and *internal evaluation*.

5.2.1.   External evaluation is that by which at the end of the studies (when the final objective or the intermediate objectives are deemed to have been achieved) the learner's attainments are appraised by reference to criteria applicable to all the learners which enable his attainments to be assigned a place in relation to the content of the learning and/or the attainments of other learners.

"Its nature (ie the nature of outside evaluation) is such as to favour standardized language teaching and courses. It focuses on the subject matter to be learned . . . The purpose is to measure results (intermediate or final)".[14]

The criteria adopted in making an evaluation of this kind are naturally defined by the teaching establishment or teacher, since the learner cannot use knowledge that he does not possess for the purpose of appraising his attainments.

In such circumstances the amount of responsibility that a learner can have in outside evaluation is extremely limited and superficial: the most he can do is to conduct for himself the tests or other means of evaluation laid down by others and perhaps correct them himself with the help of grids provided for him. Here again the only latitude he can, and should, have is to decide whether or not to submit to this kind of evaluation.

5.2.2.   Internal evaluation is the only kind, strictly speaking, that forms an integral part of the learning in the same way as the definition of objectives, contents, etc, since it is the only kind operating within the learning process, ie which is a constituent part of that process:

". . . an internal part of the learning process without which no learning can be achieved".[15]

It is one of the stages of learning, that during which the learner evaluates the attainments he has lately made as compared with what he was aiming at so that, in the first place, he can be certain that he really has acquired something — and the learning process is not at an end until this evaluation, whether positive or negative, has been carried out — and in the second place so that he can plan his subsequent learning.[16]

It is therefore a type of evaluation whose purpose, unlike that of external evaluation, is not to evaluate the learner's "linguistic ability in terms of his success in mastering course contents"[17] or by reference to the attainments of other learners but to determine to what extent the results achieved are in line with his objective.

It is this crucial evaluation,[18] centred on the learning, for which the learner must assume responsibility in self-directed learning. It is this assumption of responsibility that amounts to real self-evaluation.

[14] Porcher, L, *op cit.*

[15] Henner-Stanchina, C, and Holec, H (1977) 'Evaluation in an autonomous learning scheme' in *Mélanges Pédagogiques* CRAPEL, Nancy.

[16] For further details *cf* Henner-Stanchina, C, and Holec, H, *op cit.*

[17] Porcher, L, *op cit.*

[18] Although there may be learning without certification or external evaluation there cannot be learning without internal evaluation.

5.3.   The fundamental characteristic of self-evaluation, as well as of the definition of objectives with which it is very closely bound up, is that it integrates the learner's specific personal dimension.

5.3.1.   With regard to criteria used in evaluation, these are chosen by the learner, from all possible criteria, by reference to his own definition of the component parts of successful attainment and the relative importance thereof.

These component parts will perhaps include, for any given learner, the traditional features of correct grammar and lexical wealth, but correct pronunciation will perhaps give way to intelligibility and fluency, and 'variety of style' (making it possible to suit the performance to the mood, atmosphere, etc of the moment) may possibly be regarded as very important or indeed essential.[19] Moreover this choice need not necessarily be final: for each new step in his learning the learner may select other criteria and other combinations of them which are better suited to his new learning objective and in line with his new level of knowledge.

5.3.2.   As for the threshold by reference to which his attainments will be regarded as successful or otherwise as determined by each criterion, this will be fixed by the learner according to his own ideas of what is a satisfactory performance.

In addition, this threshold, as determined for each criterion, will not necessarily remain unchanged throughout the whole course since the learner's ideas may change as he considers one performance or another according to the objective aimed at, the level of knowledge gained, etc.

5.3.3.   Self-evaluation, ie internal evaluation carried out by the learner, represents a key-level of self-directed learning possibly even to a greater extent than does definition of objectives.

Self-directed learning that did not include acceptance of responsibility for evaluating attainments would not only be incomplete but would run the risk of rapidly becoming directed learning owing to the retroactive effect of the monitoring then exercised by the outside evaluator on the definition of objectives and the fixing of contents.[20]

5.4.   This evaluation, regarded from the standpoint of appraisal of linguistic and communicative acquisitions, is supplemented in self-directed learning by evaluation of the learning itself:

"As a language learner, one needs feedback and input information on learning strategies, learning techniques, etc, in other words, on the suitability and effectiveness of learning in relation to personal learning criteria and personal goals. This information will increase the learner's awareness of how he learns and help him make decisions as to the continuation or modification of his learning activities".[21]

This self-evaluation of learning, like that of acquisition, will be carried out on the basis of *personal criteria* such as compatibility between the proposed

---

[19] For fuller details *cf* Henner-Stanchina, C, and Holec, H, *op cit.*

[20] A number of suggestions on the exercise of self-evaluation in language are made in Oskarsson, M (1980) *Approaches to self-assessment in foreign language learning*, Pergamon, Oxford, and in Henner-Stanchina, C, and Holec, H, *op cit.*

[21] *cf* Henner-Stanchina, C, and Holec, H, *op cit.*

methods and techniques and the external constraints (availability of place and time; physical possibilities, etc) and internal constraints (intellectual and physical ability, etc) and by reference to *personal thresholds*.[2]

As a general rule it will lead the learner to evaluate how he has taken charge of his learning, from the definition of objectives and contents to selection of methods and techniques, monitoring the learning procedure and evaluating what has been acquired.

6. Conclusions

6.1.   As we come to the end of this chapter on the characterization of self-directed learning of languages, the aim of which was to indicate and express in practical form what autonomous learning is, we come up against the problem of the interdependence of the decisions made at each stage of the learning process. As we have said, the choices adopted at each of these stages are dependent on those made at other stages. This interdependence, however, operates at different levels: although definition of objectives and evaluation of what has been acquired cannot be imagined one without the other, the relationship between definition of objectives and fixing of contents is not so close, since definition of objectives governs to a very high degree the choice of contents yet does not make that choice imperative; as regards the relationship between contents on the one hand and methods and techniques on the other, although it does in fact exist in that it is not possible for no matter what sort of content to be mastered by any method whatsoever, the relationship does nevertheless come about in an asymmetrical fashion (contents must not be determined by methods, even though in reality this still happens far too often in language teaching) and on the other hand it allows a good deal of latitude for decision (a fair number of methods and techniques make it possible to acquire a given content); finally, monitoring learning procedure appears to have very little connection with the other learning levels.

6.2.   In these circumstances what can one conclude as to the possible degrees of self-direction in learning? Can we conceive of partial and supplementary degrees of acceptance of responsibility on the part of the learner, the teaching establishment or the teacher?

In theory and in practice it is only the level of the monitoring of learning procedure that can be dissociated from the rest: consequently this represents the only possible example of divided responsibility and it is not by chance that this method has come to be used in the less conventional forms of teaching and learning (distance teaching and programmed teaching).

As regards the remaining levels of learning, it is practically impossible to make different parties responsible for these — eg to let the learner assume responsibility for defining objectives and contents whilst the teacher looks after evaluation and the choice of methods and techniques; — indeed the differences in criteria adopted by the various parties would involve a danger

[22] For further details *cf* Henner-Stanchina, C, and Holec, H, *op cit*.

of imperfect adjustment of the decisions to suit different levels of learning or even that the decisions made by the institutionally stable party (the teacher) would actually dominate those of the institutionally transient party (the learner).

From this standpoint therefore there are no possible degrees of self-direction in learning.

6.3. If we can speak of degrees of self-direction in learning, this can be only in terms of the help which the learner can obtain during the time of his acceptance of responsibility. A learner who is not yet autonomous or not entirely so or is in the process of acquiring autonomy must nevertheless, as we have seen, assume responsibility for the whole of his learning although he may benefit from help given by a teacher or derived from teaching aid (*cf* learning with support). This help, which may be large or small (though without ever amounting to transfer of responsibility) consequently entails an 'alleviation' of the burden of responsibility (the component parts of which we have described in this chapter). In this sense it is then possible to distinguish different degrees of self-direction, determined by the relative proportion of decisions made with or without support.

6.4. The nature and operation of self-directed learning imply, as we have found, redefinition of the learner's role. But they also imply redefinition of the roles of the teacher and the teaching establishment. These are the implications we now propose to examine.

III. IMPLICATIONS OF SELF-DIRECTED LEARNING

1. The new role of the learner

1.1.　As pointed out by H Janne in his analysis of self-management of education, and this applies *mutatis mutandis* to self-directed language learning, acceptance of responsibility for the learning by the learner involves two fundamental changes in the context of learning: a change in the *definition of the knowledge* to be acquired and a change in the *learner/knowledge* relationship.

> "Self-management of education . . . modifies the relationship between the learner and existing 'knowledge', and on the other hand it modifies the way in which knowledge itself is built up and is developed"[23]

1.1.1.　As regards the knowledge or know-how to be acquired, although this may theoretically be defined globally, ie by considering the totality of the attainments which potentially all learners might adopt as objectives and without prejudging the choice of each of them, and objectively, ie by some party other than the learner and who would describe this knowledge or know-how by analysing the use made of it by a native speaker,[24] it cannot, however, be defined where it has reference to a particular learner. As we have seen, every learner determines his own objectives and contents by making choices based on personal criteria and from all the communication potentialities open to him and this is how he defines the knowledge or know-how he wishes to acquire. In linguistic terms each learner therefore defines the idiolect he wants to master and that idiolect cannot exist apart from him, even if its component elements are part of a language-system shared by the entire community.

Objective, universal knowledge is therefore replaced by subjective, individual knowledge.

1.1.2.　In this way the learner/knowledge relationship is completely upset; the learner is no longer faced with an 'independent' reality that escapes him, to which he cannot but give way, but with a reality which he himself constructs and dominates, even if this cannot be done in an anarchical or uncertain manner.

Note:　Let us recall here (*cf* p 13) that such a construction of a reality does not mean that the learner 'invents' a new language; he defines his idiolect by reference to observation and analysis of sources of information derived from various kinds of documents and from informants.

1.2.　In its turn this new learning context changes the learner/learning relationship. The position of passivity and dependence in which the learner was necessarily confined because the knowledge was not accessible to him without the help of an expert-teacher is no longer tenable. Freed from the

---

[23] Janne, H, *op cit*, p 24.

[24] Verbal communication in any language has an advantage over most other learning objectives in that it 'exists' in the objective reality.

need for a mediator actually possessing this knowledge, the learner is *ipso facto* freed from the need for mediatization (instruction): it is no longer essential for the learning to be taken charge of by the teacher, the learner himself can assume responsibility for it.

1.3.   This (potential) acceptance of responsibility, defining the learner's new roles (and which we have described in the previous chapter), can operate only if two conditions are fulfilled: that the learner is willing and that he is also capable of assuming responsibility.

1.3.1.   As regards the first condition it must be emphasized, with B Schwartz, that:

'participation in education in our present day societies must be learnt, does not occur automatically and is not a response to a spontaneous aspiration'.[25]

But it should also be noted that this state of things is not irreversible, its cause not being written into the history of the development of mankind.

'Many people feeling a need for education are frightened by the opportunities for participation offered to them and are too inhibited to make use of them. This is the result of their early directive schooling followed by conditioning and alienating occupational activities'.[26]

1.3.2.   The same remarks may apply as regards the second condition: few adults are capable of assuming responsibility for their learning, as proved by experience,[27] for the simple reason that they have never had occasion to use this ability. With the majority of them, therefore, autonomy has to be acquired.

In essence this acquisition will bring two different processes into play:

— a gradual *'deconditioning' process* which will cause the learner to break away, if only by putting them into words, from *a priori* judgments and prejudices of all kinds that encumber his ideas about learning languages and the role he can play in it — to free himself from the notion that there is one ideal method, that teachers possess that method, that his knowledge of his mother tongue is of no use to him for learning a second language, that his experience as a learner of other subjects, other know-how, cannot be transferred even partially, that he is incapable of making any valid assessment of his performance, and so on;

— a gradual *process of acquiring* the knowledge and know-how he needs in order to assume responsibility for his learning; to learn to use tools such as dictionaries and grammar books, to assemble and analyse a corpus, to describe his expectations in terms that will serve to define a learning process, all of which implies discovering descriptive categories which will not necessarily be those of a linguist or a professional teacher; to learn to analyse his performance, and so on.

It is through the parallel operation of these two processes that the learner will gradually proceed from a position of dependence to one of independence, from a non-autonomous state to an autonomous one.

1.3.3.   In order for the two conditions essential for actualizing the acceptance of responsibility to be brought together it is necessary, though this is perhaps

[25] Schwartz, B, CCC/EP (77) 8 revised, p 15.

[26] Schwartz, B, *ibid.*

[27] Experience also shows that there is no correlation between level of studies and autonomy.

154

not enough (*cf* Chapter V, *General conclusions*) that a new type of instruction be offered to the learner.

2. New objectives of teaching

2.1.   In a general way teaching coming under the heading of action based on autonomy should no longer be looked upon as *'producing'* learning but as *'facilitating'* it. It must take place in the shape of a set of procedures most of which are still to be discovered, procedures that help the learner to learn and not that make him learn, and which are used by the learner rather than 'mould' him.

Note: This is also fully in accord with the new concepts of foreign language learning derived from current research and according to which learning is not a passive process of stock-piling information supplied by the teaching but, on the contrary, an active, creative operation by means of which the learner converts into acquired knowledge information provided for him in an organized manner (teaching) or in non-organized form ('natural' untreated information).

This new concept of the function of teaching in learning goes very much further than the simple distinction between directive and non-directive teaching.

2.2.   As regards the teaching objectives properly speaking, these are essentially twofold:

— firstly the objective of teaching must be to help the learner acquire the linguistic and communicative abilities he has defined for himself;

— secondly the teaching must also help the learner acquire autonomy for himself, ie to learn to learn.

'To lead the learner from an initially dependent to a finally independent position should be one of the built-in educational objectives of a learning programme'.[28]

These two objectives must be pursued together in so far as, in accordance with what we have already said (*cf* p 7), it is out of the question to regard autonomy as a precondition of language learning and since it would be absurd to proceed to learn autonomy when learning of the language is finished.

This raises the problem of how far the methods adopted to achieve the first objective and to achieve the second are compatible. One example will suffice to place this problem in its right perspective: something such as 'programmed instruction' which would perhaps be suitable for helping the learner to acquire a knowledge of a language would nevertheless place him in a position of dependence and irresponsibility such as would immediately conflict with his aim of achieving autonomy.

2.3.   The practical means of organizing and operating such teaching have begun to be investigated in various pilot experiments (*cf* Chapter IV) but there is still much to be done in defining them and putting them into effect in the field of future education.

[28] *cf* Trim, J L M, *op cit.*

3. The teachers' new roles

3.1.   In a system where the learner assumes responsibility for his learning whilst still learning how to do so, where the teaching is centred on giving support to the learner, the teacher himself must also redefine his role by reference to this focusing on the learner and his learning.

Without being in a position to define exhaustively in what way teachers are to intervene in the system (but *cf* Chapter IV on current experiments and *infra*) one may anticipate that the functions of the teacher will in part still be what they sometimes are in a directed system (research into the field of foreign language acquisition, research into the field of language learning methodology, the 'supply' of authentic or organized materials, etc) but will change very considerably in the matter of 'help' and 'advice' which will constitute the support needed by a learner learning to learn at the same time as he acquires a language.[29] The teacher will have to help the learner develop his ability to:

— define his objectives, ie help him to find and use descriptive categories sufficiently 'refined' to enable him to define his learning objectives based on definition of needs; at the very least this means sensibilization to the functioning of verbal communication (by thinking about communicative behaviour in the mother tongue, for example);

— to define contents and progressions to be made, ie to help him assemble learning *corpora* and analyze them in order to extract those linguistic and communicative elements forming the subject to be learnt; at the very least this means supplying information on the possible sources of learning materials (authentic and/or didactic) and preparation for the techniques of describing and classifying linguistic information (composing card-indexes, glossaries etc);

— to choose methods and techniques, ie to help him draw up lists of learning activities and decide what use they are; this will imply developing educational competence based initially on a list of techniques in use (those suggested in different manuals, for example), then observation of his own learning behaviour, and on information regarding language learning processes for adults);

— to monitor the learning procedure, ie essentially to help him realistically to take account of constraints of all kinds that press upon him and to impose a suitable working 'discipline' upon himself;

— to evaluate what he has acquired and his learning process, ie to seek out and use personal appraisal criteria and thresholds based on personal expectations: this will imply the introduction of performance situations (encounters with native speakers, for example) and the elaboration of performance analysis tools and techniques (development of a descriptive linguistic competence, for example).

---

[29]*cf* the suggestions on the role of helper put forward by Henner-Stanchina, C (1976) in *Autonomy: A viable strategy for adult language learners* Degree thesis, University of Nancy II, and those on the tutor made by Scheffknecht, J J (1975) in *The tutor* CCC, Strasbourg.

Concurrently with this the teacher will need to help the learner to appreciate and overcome the 'conditioning' resulting from his previous learning experience which influences his ideas about learning a foreign language.

3.2. As a rule, therefore, in contrast to the apprehension often created by the concept of autonomy in learning, the teacher will find his role becomes more varied rather than curtailed, strengthened rather than weakened (not in terms of authority but in terms of competence) and much greater demands will be made on his creativity than on his highly developed knowledge of teaching techniques. The traditional teacher who might have been regarded as 'replaceable' (*cf* teaching machines) will give way to a teacher whose role in the process of developing the learner will be irreplaceable. His status will no longer be based on the power conferred by hierarchical authority but on the quality and importance of his relationship to the learner.

3.3. This new definition of the teacher's functions will of course give rise to an acute problem concerning training, particularly in the immediate future, but it will also give rise to others of an institutional nature that are just as practical and urgent:

". . . will there be a high proportion of *full-time* educators, or will there be a majority of experts, counsellors, consultants and assistants, all *part-time?* What qualifications will be required in either case? How much importance will be attached to experience? How will qualifications be awarded and classed? . . .[30]

These are all questions to which answers will have to be found when we have got past the stage of the experimental introduction of self-directed learning systems and in the light of those experiences.

4. Conclusions: structural consequences

There are two overall educational situations that will arise in the future:

4.1. The first situation will be that in which autonomous learners will find themselves (whether this autonomy has been achieved 'naturally' or 'systematically'). For such the learning structure will from the outset need to be a self-directed one, organized therefore by reference to their specific learning needs. It may be imagined that in a structure of this sort there will be a large and assorted body of informants of all kinds, both human and technical and that there will be a technological infrastructure capable of temporarily making up for deficiencies in individual technological means, etc.

4.2. However, the most prevalent situation will be that of learners who are not yet autonomous but are involved in the process of acquiring the ability to assume responsibility for their learning.

In this situation the learning structure will be made up of a maximum (as regards quantity and variety) of both human and technical supports.

4.3. In both these situations, however, it will be essential for the learning structure regularly to supply the learners with all the information that will be of benefit to them in their learning, whether they be autonomous or not:

[30]Janne, H, *op cit*, p 18.

— information on language needs in the world outside (in society) such as may be needed by a learner when making decisions as to his objectives;

— information on the processes of acquiring second languages such as will help the learner to arrive at a better definition of his methods and techniques and his learning procedure;

— information on verbal communication, the psychological and social dimensions of which need to be considered by a learner when defining objectives and evaluation processes;

— information on available documentation which the learner will use for defining contents.

It will thus be necessary to set up systems that are both very diversified, in order to take into account the broad range of knowledge, and very dynamic in order to keep pace with the development of this knowledge and of the world outside. It is in this direction also that consideration and research will need to move in the years ahead if we wish to develop autonomous learning.

At present, a number of more or less comprehensive experiments concerning the autonomy of learning have already been launched. We shall describe some of these experiments in the next chapter in order, if possible, to single out some hypothetical models that could form the basis for future learning systems.

COUNCIL
OF EUROPE

CONSEIL
DE L' EUROPE

6 CHAPTER SIX: 6
EVALUATION

INTRODUCTION TO CHAPTER SIX

Evaluation is an essential component of language learning systems. Actually, it would be more correct to say that it is an assembly of different components. As John Trim points out in the first extract, evaluation has a variety of roles to play in the learning process and may be carried out in numerous ways, the most appropriate ways to be determined in each case in accordance with its purpose and the particular circumstances.

In the second extract Mats Oskarsson focuses on self-assessment, describing its possible roles and presenting various forms it may take.

from an original paper by J L M Trim

THE PLACE OF TESTING, ASSESSMENT AND EVALUATION IN COMMUNICATIVE LANGUAGE LEARNING SYSTEMS DEVELOPMENT

1. Why test?

Testing, assessment and evaluation are necessary aspects of a language-learning system. As such they have formed part of the programme of systems development set out by the Council of Europe Modern Languages Project from its earliest days. Nevertheless, the group of experts charged in 1971 with investigating the feasibility of a European unit/credit scheme for foreign language learning by adults decided not to concern itself immediately with these aspects, feeling that the first priority lay with the specification of objectives. There seemed to be a distinct danger that the premature involvement of the formidable expertise of the institutions engaged in language testing and examining might lead to definitions of language learning objectives being determined, not by the communicative needs of learners, but rather by what the professionals believed to be testable by their existing techniques and in accordance with their received criteria. This is not to disparage testing expertise, which is based on long practical experience and must be respected. However, the tail must not wag the dog. Priority attaches to the clear formulation of objectives. As Porcher pointed out to the Ludwigshafen symposium: 'Evaluation has meaning only in relation to the teaching objectives to which it is applied; reciprocally an objective does not really exist unless its definition includes its own evaluation criteria. If these two reciprocal and complementary conditions are not met, a teaching programme is not worthy of the name ... In our field, as in others, the first step must be an operational description of objectives, not a general discourse on vague aims. Determining the goal is essential and this involves deciding what a learner *must be capable of* by the end of his learning experience. Expressed in these terms, an objective includes, in its definition, the very means for evaluating it.'

If we agree that evaluation is closely related to objectives specification, we can readily see that it can perform a variety of functions in a language programme, for instance:

Placement testing attempts to establish what the learner is already able to do with respect to the language and also his study skills, learner-type and language aptitude. The aim is to ensure that the learner meets the prerequisites for following a given programme, or is routed to an appropriate programme, or allocated to an appropriate group, etc.;

Progress testing gives information to the learner and teacher as to whether learning is taking place as planned, so that the programme can be modified or different options exercized, eg remedial work, accelerated programmes, changed modalities, etc;

Achievement testing ascertains whether the learner has achieved the terminal course objectives. This information is valuable to learners for motivational reasons, and for planning their next step, and to teachers and course planners in assessing the overall success, and particular strengths and weaknesses, of the programme so that it can be amended for future use.

These purposes all relate to a particular course, and are of primary concern to the teachers and students directly involved. Other tests are designed to give information to interested parties outside the immediate teaching/learning situation. These may be (1) national authorities concerned with the output of a national education system as part of accountability for the use of resources and the maintenance of comparability to ensure justice to individuals and groups; (2) potential employers and other users of trained linguists; (3) institutions of higher and further education recruiting nationally and interested in ensuring that entry standards are met and can be presupposed of students; (4) the teachers and learners immediately involved, as a means of evaluating their own achievements against wider norms and criteria. External tests or examinations may measure the achievement of objectives specified in curricular guidelines or in explicit national defined syllabuses. Alternatively, specific objectives may not be set. Instead, the *proficiency* of candidates may be tested by eliciting language behaviour from candidates and evaluating it either in relation to the performance of other candidates (*norm referencing*) or against some agreed evaluative criteria (*criterion referencing*). These two principles may of course also be employed in achievement, progress and placement testing.

2. What to test?

Since the Council of Europe Modern Languages Programme emphasizes language learning as a prerequisite for a much wider movement of people and ideas among member states, it focuses on the use of language for communication. Communication may take place directly, in face-to-face (or 'ear-to-ear', ie telephonic) interaction, or indirectly, through communication media (newspapers, books, films, recordings, radio, TV, public announcements, etc). In both cases, a message is formulated, encoded and produced by a sender, transmitted by means of some medium, and perceived, identified, understood and interpreted by a receiver. For communication to be effective, both parties draw on their understanding of the language concerned as a symbolic system (linguistic competence) and the conventions governing its use (communicative competence) as well as their understanding of the extra-linguistic parameters of the situation (including background knowledge) in which the message is embedded, together with the principles of social interaction (social competence).

In addition to these different aspects of knowledge or 'competence', the language user must have developed the mental and physical skills necessary to act as sender or receiver. In indirect communication an individual is called upon to act only as one or the other. In direct communication the rapid switching (and to some extent overlapping) of roles make further demands. In general, productive skills, involving stimulus-free recall, are more demanding than receptive recognition skills. Neither knowledge nor skills are ends in themselves, but prerequisites for effective communicative action in pursuit of social goals in given situations.

Language testing may then be directed towards:

1. Establishing that the learner has acquired the requisite competences:

a. Linguistic – phonological, lexical, morphological and syntactic categories, forms, structures and rules and their associated meanings);

b. Communicative (functional and notional categories, pragmatics, rules of usage);

c. Social (background, socio-cultural knowledge, principles of social interaction).

2. Establishing that the learner has acquired the component skills of language production and reception.

3. Establishing that the learner is able in fact to participate effectively in communicative acts as sender, receiver or interactively.

3. How to test?

While these categories can be distinguished in principle, to do so in practice presents problems. The effective performance of communicative tasks presupposes competences and skills, but is not equal to their mere sum. Attestation of knowledge will not guarantee skill. Attestation of skill will not guarantee effective communication. Direct tests of communication are difficult to conduct in accordance with recognized test criteria. These are:

a. Validity: that the test actually tests what it purports to test. We may distinguish *face validity* – the test not only tests what it purports to test but is clearly seen to do so by candidates and teachers – from *correlational validity* – the test does not directly test what it purports to test, but measures more conveniently some other factor which can be shown to correlate highly with what is being tested.

b. Reliability: that the test administered to the same candidates on different occasions and marked by the same examiners would produce the same result.

c. Discrimination: that the test produces a well-spread distribution of results, enabling candidates to be placed in rank order. A test which produces 'bunching' (ie a large proportion of candidates with similar scores) is held to lack discrimination. This occurs if a test is too easy (bunching at the top end) or too difficult (bunching at the bottom end), but also if a normal distribution curve results, but with a narrow standard deviation.

d. Feasibility: that the test can be administered efficiently given the available material and human resources.

e. Positive backwash: that the test promotes or encourages desirable educational practices rather than undesirable ones (negative backwash).

Clearly, these criteria are frequently in conflict. Which are to be regarded as of greater importance depends upon the function of the test. For instance as a test of general proficiency, a well-devised dictation has high correlational validity, reliability, discrimination and feasibility. It has low face validity and negative backwash. Consequently, it is highly regarded by testing technicians and administrators but rejected by educationists as dull, mechanical, demotivating and unrealistic. In contrast, group role-play tests have high face validity and highly positive backwash. They tend to have low reliability and present problems in feasibility. They are consequently favoured by class teachers, but an object of suspicion to technical experts and administrators. Consequently, a suitable dictation is useful in placement testing but problematic in public terminal examinations. Group role play is useful in progress testing, but also problematic in public examinations.

Irrespective of the purposes of tests (which often overlap), there is a varied (and sometimes variable) terminology which refers to the techniques of testing. For example, so-called objective tests are usually those which, it is claimed, can be scored or marked without any dispute as to the correct answer. Often these employ *multiple-choice* questions, *true/false* questions or *cloze techniques*. However, it should be noted that the means of eliciting responses (or the choice of questions provided) is not necessarily objective, since they may depend on the personal views of the test constructor about the structure of language itself and the nature of the skills involved in using it.

For practical purposes, the effectiveness of any educational test depends on its *sampling* procedures, and these present special difficulties in language tests. No test can measure the full extent of a student's skill or knowledge of a language, so it must rely on selecting tasks or items which are assumed to be representative. This may be by a 'global' test of performance, as often used in conventional examinations, or by attempting to isolate and separately measure what are assumed, for test purposes, to be discrete skills, as in many objective type tests. However, some of the traditional assumptions about the nature of skills in language are not always helpful. For example, the conventional idea of 'four skills' – hearing, speaking, reading and writing – can be very misleading, since each of these actually represents a mode of using a language which employs many interlocking and overlapping sub-skills. Thus a test of reading at a very elementary level may be primarily one of word recognition; at an advanced level it will involve a knowledge of syntax, vocabulary and of the subject of a passage to be understood. Moreover, most communicative activities involve participants in both productive and receptive activities. Discrete skill testing may reduce, quite deliberately, one side of a communication to triviality, thus destroying the authenticity – and indeed the whole point – of the communication.

At advanced levels it becomes increasingly difficult to isolate measurable skills and to establish their relative weight in any 'overall command' of the language. Assumptions about what is 'correct', in terms of pronunciation or grammar, also become less helpful as proficiency increases, since knowing a language then becomes more clearly the ability to communicate, using an extended range of linguistic features, rather than being able to make the 'right' noises or even use particular words. This may explain the anomaly of the native speaker being 'permitted' to commit errors which are sometimes penalized in the foreign learner. While specific tests of pronunciation, grammar, vocabulary etc may be highly valid at one level of language learning, they may be less so at another. For test purposes, criteria of language performance do not remain the same at all levels of learning.

Test types

A very large number of test types is now available. James and Rouve, in their *Survey of Curricula and Performance* (1973) list 128. No one test type can properly satisfy all criteria and cover the range of knowledge, skills and communicative activities which constitute the learner's objective. It is necessary to examine each type to establish its strengths and weaknesses, and on the basis of the resultant test typology to assemble balanced and feasible test batteries.

The Council of Europe approach has been based on the contention that a proper assessment of the communicative needs of a particular target group, given the characteristics of the learners and the resources (especially time) available to them, it is possible to arrive at (a) the specification of the communication situations in which they will have to participate, (b) how likely they are to be called upon to act in those situations, and hence (c) the functional, notional and linguistic content of their learning, as well as the skills required.

The various Threshold Level specifications (now developed for English, French, German, Spanish, Italian, Danish, Swedish, Dutch and Catalan) are the result of the application of these principles and criteria to the needs of those learners, probably the largest single group, who wish to be able to meet the basic demands of everyday social interaction. As such, it may be an appropriate basis for the syllabus of new Diplomas and Certificates for foreign learners of European languages. The Threshold Level has already been used, flexibly, in this way when introducing or revising a number of examinations of English, French and German as foreign languages, both for adults and in the school system.

4. The specimen threshold level test

In accordance with the various principles and criteria outlined above, a specimen Threshold Level test for English was developed by Dr P Groot (Utrecht) and Mr A Harrison (London). The content and format of the tests included are set out in the attached schedule. The test has been extensively piloted, and psychometric data are available. The test materials are available for consultation by groups interested in experimentation or the development of new examinations. In addition, other studies by Council of Europe experts on testing problems at Threshold Level can be made available.

5. Who tests?

Evaluation is to be seen, not as a means of imposing the objectives of an authoritarian technocracy upon the population of learners, but as a means of enabling learners to achieve more effectively more *objectives* corresponding to their *needs*. This necessitates a close interaction between learners, teachers, planners and experts at all levels and stages in the educational process, in order to encourage an optimal autonomy of the learner, but within a properly supportive framework. External persons, teachers, the group of learners and the individual learner all have their proper roles to play.

Unassisted self-evaluation by the individual learner is most reliable when he is faced with tasks which involve a straightforward judgement of right and wrong, and student errors can be predicted. The education of the learner to make reliable and valid autonomous judgements on the effectiveness of his communication is a necessary part of the learning process. He may, for example, be provided with appropriate models, ways of establishing links between his needs and immediate learning objectives, which he may be able to formulate more realistically as a result of being better able to evaluate his own performance, progress and possibilities. It is important to develop a supportive role of learner groups which can give the individual the feeling of sharing his problems and difficulties with others and arriving at an agreement on joint remedial work; in particular, pronunciation and fluency problems are better placed in a group context than identified and tackled on an individual level. Work in groups is useful for developing an awareness of criteria and self-identification with group objectives. Impressionistic judgements by group members on each other's communication, even if they are unreliable, can be useful, since in the dialectics of discussion awareness of criteria is further sharpened. Moreover, the inhibitory effect of feedback of errors can be mitigated by a positive group dynamics. In this respect it is necessary that teachers should receive guidance on psychological problems raised by evaluation in a group context.

Teacher evaluation becomes necessary whenever there are errors arising from structural conflict (formal, semantic, pragmatic and cultural) which are removed from the consciousness of the learner. Monitoring and recognition of self-evaluation by the teacher is also valuable. External evaluation may be advisable when general social recognition of achievement is involved together with the establishment of equivalences, nationally and internationally.

If this is true for the choice of goals and methods, it is also true for evaluation: the point of testing is to give information to the student, and also to others for their mutual benefit, about his standing in relation to his appropriate learning. The range of possible evaluations is wide, from an apparently unassailable, objectively validated grade (pass or fail) with international currency to a momentary expression (smile or frown) on the face of the teacher. Thus the roles of parties involved vary according to situations and requirements, as illustrated in Fig. 1.

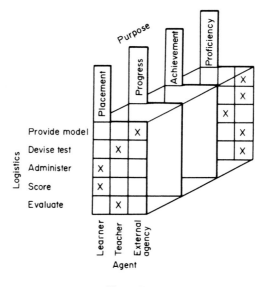

Figure 1

One area which needs to be explored and cultivated in the jungle of possible forms of evaluation is how the individual student may be brought to an efficient realization of his own achievement, or lack of it, in relation to the goals he sets himself in the first place. This is one kind of evaluation which is particularly important for the adult learner, who may well be highly motivated, but needs this motivation reinforced by practical applications and feedback at frequent intervals, preferably timed according to his own demands. This requires that he should have available to him not only means of assessing his own performance, but also means of learning how to make the necessary assessments. Dr Oskarsson's study is an important first step, an exploration of several possible forms of self-assessment for use in adult language learning.

Tests: content & format

	content	format	time	ability measures
Listening	(all 3 listening tests recorded on tape cassette)			
1	conversation between man and woman on general topics	15 sections, + 1 multiple choice item on each section	13 mins	understanding conversation (as a necessary condition for joining in)
2	directions to places on a map	writing figures 1–5 on map in test booklet, to show places indicated by directions given	3 mins	understanding spoken directions
3	questions and answers on personal details (name, address, etc) for filling a form	writing in the test booklet the information given	2½ mins	writing down information heard, including some spelled out
Reading				
1	text of advertisement	passage + 5 multiple choice items		understanding information read, including factual, persuasive and personal material
2	text of leaflet	passage + 5 multiple choice items		
3	part of letter	passage + 15 true/false items	20 mins	
Writing	stimulus material provided as the basis for writing a letter	background information + 5 items to be conveyed in writing	20 mins	expressing specified information in writing
Speaking	(individual test) stimulus material (speech, pictures, written text) provided as the basis for taking part in a conversation	18 questions, then 5 items for role-playing	6–10 mins	expressing specified information and appropriate reactions in speech

167

from M Oskarsson, *Approaches to self-assessment in foreign language learning*

1. INTRODUCTION

1.1 Introductory remarks on the role of evaluation within a European unit/credit system for modern language learning by adults

It has been recognized that evaluation within the unit/credit system will require many and varied testing techniques. An early symposium on 'linguistic content, means of evaluation and their interaction in the teaching and learning of modern languages in adult education' (Rüschlikon, May 1971) reached the conclusion that 'as the mastery of a foreign language, even at a fairly low level, is too complex a matter for evaluation to be based only on objective techniques, *both objective and subjective assessment must be employed*' (our italics) (Council of Europe document, 1971, p. 4). In a paper presented on the same occasion Kingsbury (1971) remarked that 'if assessment within units is to be truly effective, then most certainly *a multiplicity of assessment techniques will have to be employed* (our italics). If a system of continuous assessment is applied, one must recognize that continuous assessment is applied; one must also recognize that continuous assessment does not mean simply a series of formal tests given at irregular intervals' (p 6). At the symposium on 'A European unit/credit system for modern language learning by adults' at Ludwigshafen in 1977 the participants jointly recommended that 'effective evaluation tools, ranging from self-assessment instruments to standardized tests for defined objectives' (Council of Europe document, 1977, p 4) be developed.

Accordingly, we will assume that a wide range of evaluation procedures and test types will be needed in order to achieve the 'multi-faceted learning system adapted to their (ie the learners') individual needs and objectives' (Trim, 1973, p 1) which is the project's aim.

The importance of involving the learner in the question of evaluation has also been repeatedly emphasized in Council of Europe documents dealing with the unit/credit project:

> 'It was felt strongly that the student should be given a greater responsibility for determining the pace of his own learning and should be involved wherever possible in the process of evaluation' (Conclusions, *Rüschlikon Symposium*; see Council of Europe document, 1971, p 4).

> 'With regard to the European unit/credit system for language learning, it is essential to find an appropriate instrument to evaluate the communicative ability of the learner and help him develop a self-critical awareness of his acquisition of knowledge, so that he can find his place in the continuous learning process within the framework of a unit/credit system' (Conclusions, *St Wolfgang Symposium*: see Council of Europe document, 1973, p 9).

> 'In an adult education system, student control of the training process should be extended to evaluation procedures, and exercised in different ways according to the functions – whether educational, scientific or social – which evaluation is expected to perform' (Leon, 1976, p 1).

> 'The education of the learner to make reliable and valid autonomous judgements on the effectiveness of his communication is a necessary part of the learning process' (Council of Europe document, 1976, p 7).

'A European language policy of this kind should be designed so as to serve the basic ideals of the Council for Cultural Cooperation such as:
to make the process of language learning more democratic by providing the conceptual tools for the planning, construction and conduct of courses closely geared to the needs, motivations and characteristics of the learner, and enabling him so far as possible to steer and control his own progress (Trim, 1977, p 1).

Engaging the learner actively in the evaluation of learning effects will probably lead to greater interest in techniques for continuous assessment, as opposed to terminal or 'end-of-unit' assessment, which is emphasized in traditional testing. This does not mean that assessment by the learner himself is entirely different in purpose from formal outside testing. The general trend towards self-management in adult education is sometimes taken to include evaluation aspects as well, so that even decisions concerning adequate initial standards for a particular field of study may be made by the learner himself on the basis of self-administered tests (*cf* for example Section 3.3).

In principle, self-assessment can thus be both *terminal* (or *summative* in the terminology of Bloom, Hastings, and Madaus, 1971) and *continuous*, although it is very seldom practised for the former purpose. By tradition, terminal evaluation is what we have formal tests and central testing institutions for, as it were. Assessment by the learner himself has typically been regarded as synonymous with 'formative exercises' belonging to the student's practice book. It is only quite recently, as a result of the increased demands for needs-oriented, learner-centred education, that a new attitude towards language testing has begun to emerge. There is a growing feeling that tests ought to be integrated into the learning process, chiefly in order to provide feedback on progress to the learner, and that they ought to be controlled, where feasible, by the learners to a greater extent than is now the case. Rivers (1973) expresses this standpoint in the following words:

'Instead of better comparative [ie norm-referenced] tests, we should seek for a better system of establishing criteria consistent with the student's personal aims and purposes, a system in which the student himself would be involved, so that his progress would be clear, at any point, and continuous. The test as an extra activity then becomes largely superfluous, unless students request it for the pleasure of demonstrating their achievement. When students enjoy tests as a challenge and an opportunity for displaying what they know, we shall have reached the optimal form and timing of the test' (pp 31–32).

This was probably written with college and university students in mind, but it does apply in the field of adult language learning as well. Many, if not most, adults who participate in courses do so because they want to satisfy their desire to learn something, not because they need, or attach great importance to, a certain formal attestation of their performance. Most of those who pursue foreign language studies purely for their own personal satisfaction usually do not have general education in their own language beyond compulsory school requirements and ordinarily they have no plans to raise their *formal* qualification levels by embarking on a comprehensive further education 'venture'. Moreover, as has been pointed out by Gorosch (1970), for instance, 'Adults who have reached a certain position in life, are rather sensitive to formal evaluation in language proficiency, particularly that concerning oral skill, knowing that the latter is rather difficult to acquire with age' (p 19).

The most important function of tests and evaluation within the unit/credit system, and indeed in any learner-centred language learning system, is consequently to provide constant diagnostically oriented feedback to the learner as he tackles the various components, or units, of the course work. In this perspective, terminal evaluation for control or accreditation purposes is only of secondary importance.

As the quotations above show, there is fairly common agreement among experts on the need for a wide variety of continuous assessment techniques, but the problems involved have not yet been solved. Discussing this question, Clark (1972) remarks that 'Although most proponents of individual instruction seem to appreciate the role and necessity for intensive formative testing in connection with individualized programmes, little substantial progress has been made yet toward resolving a number of practical measurement problems inherent in such an undertaking' (p 227). Others have warned against the dangers that may lurk in the continuous assessment approach if applied unjudiciously. Gorosch (1971), for instance, expresses concern for the possible mental stress that might result from continuous assessment, because 'it might well cause the same nervous pressure, but on more occasions than the traditional system of final examinations' (p 11). It might also be difficult to combine self-instruction and continuous assessment, he feels.

In summarizing, it may be said that a wide variety of assessment techniques will obviously be needed in order to accomplish the flexible learner-centred system which is foreseen in the unit/credit project. It also seems clear that self-assessment of the results of learning is going to be an increasingly important feature of the system and that it is necessary to make provision for the development of evaluation techniques which can be put in the hands of the learners. The most important function of such self-assessment techniques ought to be to give the individual *continuous feedback* on what he has learnt. Ideally self-assessment procedures should also enable the learner to assess his *total achievement at the end of a course* or course unit.

In this study, the emphasis is not on continuous self-assessment, since the necessary framework for experimentation in this field, ie a concrete threshold level *course*, has not yet been developed. In the opinion of the group of experts on evaluation, however, priority should be given to work on continuous assessment practices as soon as such a course becomes available.

1.2 Aims of the study

The aim of the present study is to outline possible forms of guided self-assessment in adult language learning and to suggest steps that might be taken in order to further develop methods judged to be suitable for use within the unit/credit project. The report includes a review of relevant literature and research activities, a survey of practices in various educational institutions in Scandinavia and elsewhere, concrete suggestions for self-assessment materials, and a description of field experiments with those materials. Finally, proposals for further research and practical development work are made.

4. CONCRETE SUGGESTIONS

4.1 Introduction

Broadly speaking, self-assessment is a new field in language testing and consequently there is very little accumulated knowledge and experience to draw on for our purposes. Therefore this section of the report is necessarily of a tentative and provisional nature. It is intended to suggest lines along which further research and development work seems to be most likely to yield fruitful results, rather than to present detailed and final material for immediate use by others. Failing solid experience on which to base our appreciation of the techniques proposed, further elaboration and experimentation will certainly be needed.

Possible ways of introducing the notion of self-assessment in the regular school setting will on the whole be left out. Suffice it to say that self-assessment in its simplest form consists of informal discussions between teacher and pupil about performance and grades. The pupil can, for instance, be asked to indicate his relative position in the class or in the group according to his own estimate (*cf* quotation from Upshur, 1975, in Section 4.2), or he can be asked to describe what he feels to be his language skill in concrete operational terms.

In principle, the methods outlined on the following pages could also be used in the compulsory school system, but they have primarily been devised with adults in mind.

4.2 Self-assessment by means of standardized forms

4.2.1 Global assessment

One way of giving the learner a better basis for his own assessment of language skills is to provide him with various kinds of standardized forms which rely on the learner's ability to make over-all impressionistic and introspective judgements. As has been observed from time to time, even objective, well-constructed and standardized language tests seldom tell the whole truth, just as it can be said that even the most subjective estimate always contains some truth. Discussing subjective and objective aspects of language testing Upshur (1975) reports a case where it was found that the best way to measure someone's oral proficiency was simply to ask him how well he spoke the language. The author comments:

> 'This is not very surprising. I think most of us could give a pretty accurate appraisal of our own abilities in other languages that we know. And certainly it is the rare student in a small audiolingual class who cannot tell which of his classmates are poorer and which are better than he is' (p 329).

We will start, therefore, by looking at some subjective assessment forms which are based on the hypothesis that most learners have a certain capacity for determining their own language ability – provided they have at their disposal a measuring standard by which they may express their intuitions. Assessment forms of this kind have been used in various contexts and for various purposes (see for instance Andersson, 1969, and Balke-Aurell, 1977).

A model of a very simple standard form is illustrated in *Figure 2*. It consists of a ten-point scale (or a scale with any arbitrary number of points) ranging from complete mastery of the skill in question down to no ability at all. Only those two 'anchor points' are described verbally. The learner is instructed to put a cross in the box which he feels corresponds to his proficiency level. The text is given in the learner's native language (ie German for native German learners, French for native French learners, etc) in order to avoid mistakes due to insufficient knowledge of the target language.

Figure 2: Example of self-assessment form (listening comprehension), type A

[To be translated into the learner's native language]

Instructions: Put a cross in the boxes corresponding to your estimated level in each of the four skills (LISTENING, SPEAKING, READING, WRITING).

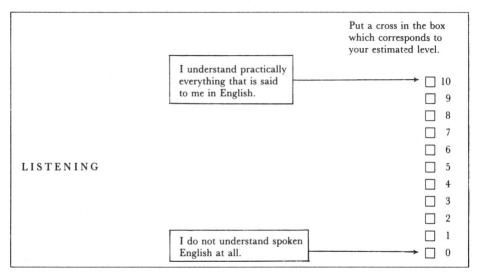

A set of four forms of this kind, one for each of the four language skills, could be used as a point of departure for discussions about the learner's command of the language. A set of guiding principles would of course have to be spelled out. The discussions could be between the learner and his teacher or between the learner and his fellow students. In both cases the procedure will result in valuable information to the learner.

Naturally enough this particular kind of form can yield only very rough estimates of stages of learning and cannot be used for assessment of learning in very restricted contexts. On the other hand, it is no doubt feasible to adapt the model to suit specific learning objectives as well. Instead of assessment in relation to the global concept 'Listening comprehension' one might for instance use 'Understanding an English news broadcast on the radio', 'Reading an English daily paper' or even 'Re-telling a story recently read in the textbook'.

It would be desirable to experiment with self-assessment materials of this kind in order to determine their usefulness. In the opinion of some experts very little faith can be put in measuring-instruments of this type. However, only controlled experiments can give us an indication of the extent to which they can be usefully employed for evaluation purposes.

4.2.2 Concrete situations

To the type A non-defined scale one can also supply descriptions of concrete situations each of which requires mastery of a particular language skill. An example of such a form (self-assessment form, type B) is shown in *Figure 3*. Again the text should be in the learner's native language, not in the language the learner is studying.

Figure 3: Example of self-assessment form (speaking), type B

SPEAKING

Imagine that you meet an English-speaking person who does not know anything about Sweden. He wants to have as much information as possible about Sweden and therefore asks you questions about living conditions, housing, nature, weather, eating habits, leisure, holidays, sport, radio and television, the royal family, celebrities, etc.

To what degree would you be able to answer his questions?

I would be able to answer his questions without any difficulties at all. → ☐	10
☐	9
☐	8
☐	7
☐	6
☐	5
☐	4
☐	3
☐	2
☐	1
I would not be able to say anything. → ☐	0

Box 10 in these scales would correspond to native proficiency and Box 0, of course, to no proficiency at all. The *Threshold Level* as it is now conceived could probably be placed at either Box 2 or Box 3, and the *Waystage* level at 1 or 2.

The situations chosen should require as little specialized factual knowledge as possible, so as to ensure that the response does not unduly reflect the learner's 'knowledge of the world' rather than actual linguistic competence.

As is all too well known in the profession, one thing that mars language teaching today is the fact that it is so notoriously difficult to produce valid and practicable oral proficiency tests (for a discussion of the problems involved, see Clark, 1972). The continuing shift in emphasis towards communicative objectives has highlighted the problem. In view of this, and in view of the fact that the unit/credit system is conceived of as essentially a system for the development of aural/oral skills, it might be worthwhile making particular efforts to develop this administratively simple approach to measuring oral communicative competence. It would seem to be possible to link the description of concrete situations quite closely to threshold level objectives, for instance. A student who has studied a *Threshold Level* course could evaluate himself in relation to the behavioural specification of 'Topics' (van Ek, 1975, Chapter 8) in this manner, using, for instance, item 5.3, which says that the learner should be able to 'characterize countries, places and regions, say something about their size, where they are situated and in what surroundings, mention possibilities for sight-seeing; seek similar information from others, what to visit and how'. Empirical data on where students who have reached *Threshold Level* place themselves on the scale, on average, would be the norm against which the individual student checks his own estimate.

Figure 3a contains a specimen form for one of the four skills (adaptations of similar forms in Balke-Aurell, 1977). They have been used for experimental purposes in a few groups of adult students.

Figure 3a: Example of self-assesement form (speaking), type B

SPEAKING		
	I would be able to answer his questions without any difficulties at all.	→ ☐ 10
		☐ 9
Imagine that you meet an English-speaking person who does not know anything about Sweden. He wants to have as much information as possible about Sweden and therefore asks you questions about living conditions, housing, nature, weather, eating habits, leisure, holidays, sport, radio and television, the royal family, celebrities, etc.		☐ 8
		☐ 7
		☐ 6
		☐ 5
		☐ 4
		☐ 3
		☐ 2
To what degree would you be able to answer his questions?		☐ 1
	I would not be able to say anything.	→ ☐ 0

4.2.3 Descriptive rating scales

In most cases it would be more fruitful, and easier for the learner, to use forms in which all points on the scale are defined in concrete terms. A non-language-specific and comprehensive form of this kind, including all four language skills, has been worked out and used in pilot experiments (self-assessment form, type C). It is illustrated in *Figure 4* (one skill only). This type of form, too, ought to be written in the learner's native language.

With the help of such aids it ought to be possible for the learner to form a rough, or maybe even a fairly accurate opinion of his level of learning. The complete set of forms, comprising all four language skills, of course makes it possible to define an approximate learning profile as well.

The forms were used in a few experiments and were then modified to include non-defined half-steps between the defined levels. It is illustrated for one skill in *Figure 4a*.

The specification of levels in any scale of this kind is problematic. The more levels there are, the more difficult it is to define each step. For our particular purposes (ie self-evaluation by unsophisticated learners) it was not judged possible to distinguish

Figure 4: Example of self-assessment form (speaking), type C (first version)

Form for self-assessment of language proficiency

Instructions: Put a cross in the boxes corresponding to your level in each of the four skills (LISTENING, SPEAKING, READING, WRITING). Only one cross for each skill!

SPEAKING	
☐ I speak the language as well as a well-educated native	5
☐ I speak the language fluently and for the most part correctly. I have a large vocabulary, so I seldom have to hesitate or search for words. On the other hand I am not completely fluent in situations in which I have had no practice with the language.	4
☐ I can make myself understood in most everyday situations, but my language is not without mistakes and sometimes I cannot find the words for what I want to say. It is difficult for me to express myself in situations in which I have had no opportunity to practise the language. I can give a short summary of general information that I have received in my native language.	3
☐ I can make myself understood in simple everyday situations, for example asking and giving simple directions, asking and telling the time, asking and talking about simpler aspects of work and interests. My vocabulary is rather limited, so it is only by a great deal of effort that I can use the language in new and unexpected situations. I am sometimes misunderstood because of faulty pronunciation and using words wrongly.	2
☐ I can just about express very simple things concerning my own situation and my nearest surroundings, for example asking and answering very simple questions about the time, food, housing, and directions. I only have a command of very simple words and phrases.	1
☐ I do not speak the language at all.	0

clearly, in easily understood terms, between more than six levels (including the zero and full proficiency levels). An experienced evaluator, on the other hand, may be able to use a more elaborate scale comprising a larger number of defined levels.

The content of the descriptions is of course crucial. Ideally different learners should understand them in the same way, but this cannot be taken for granted. From a psychological point of view it would further be preferable to exclude negative definitions such as 'sometimes I cannot find the words for what I want to say' in favour of consistent positive wording, but then the explicitness would probably suffer. It is considerably easier to establish a distinct hierarchy of levels if one is allowed to use both positive and negative statements.

It might be possible to link this kind of descriptive scale to formal tests, such as the *Threshold Level* test, by establishing rough equivalences between scale levels and test scores. In order to do this one would need to administer the self-assessment scale together with the test to a sizeable group of students representing different stages of learning. By such a procedure it would further be possible to relate scale levels to other defined levels of performance. Some work of this kind has been carried out in Sweden; rough comparisons between scale levels and stages in the Swedish school system can be made.

With slight modification these self-assessment scales could be used for the rating of others or as a general framework in language teaching contexts. Instead of using the first person singular in the defining statements ('I can . . .':, etc), impersonal constructions would be used.

It has to be emphasized, however, that the primary aim of the present scales is to provide *learners* with a global self-assessment tool. For other purposes there are of course other scales available as well (*cf* for instance, Trim 1977, in which John Trim also discusses the general usefulness of generalized performance ratings).

One final, but very important, point ought to be made. It concerns the need for training. In order to be successful in the use of subjective self-assessment materials of the kind discussed here most learners would need some practice in the use of the techniques involved. Otherwise there is a risk that personality factors may influence, or even invalidate, the results obtained (see further Section 4.5). Proper training in self-observation and in making judgements ought to be made part of the learning process.

4.3 Assessment in relation to individual goals

4.3.1 *Individual goals and individualized instruction*

One of the main purposes of the planned unit/credit scheme is to develop a learner-centred and flexible instructional system which can cater to individual needs:

'A unit/credit system of this kind appears to offer a promising framework for guidance combined with freedom and flexibility in the at present badly understructured field of adult education.'

The shift of emphasis from the teaching process itself to individual differences in modes and strategies of learning, to differences in learning goals, and to behavioural objectives, is accompanied by a redirection of interest from norm-referenced tests, ie tests where the learner's performance is matched against that of other learners, to criterion-referenced tests, where the learner's performance is evaluated in relation to some predetermined criteria, ideally concrete language behaviours (*cf* for instance Steiner, 1974). The latter type of test has the advantage that 'matching against the criterion becomes a challenge and a guide to further effort' (Rivers, 1973, p 28) instead of 'a hurdle to be surmounted'. Rivers goes on to say that in using criterion-referenced tests 'the student knows exactly what knowledge he must demonstrate and either demonstrates it and moves on or cannot demonstrate it and goes back to see how he can improve his performance'. The explicitness of performance objectives of the kind embodied in the unit/credit model likewise makes for greater clarity and 'gives all those involved in the teaching/learning process, including the learner himself, a clear view of just what is expected of them' (van Ek, 1975, p 22).

Criterion-referenced tests and performance objectives thus facilitate the adaptation of instruction to individual goals, and the learner can assume more responsibility for his own training, so that 'when he feels ready to match the criterion, he tests. Note that he tests: it is not we who test him. If necessary, he later retests. When satisfied that he has matched the criterion, he moves on' (Rivers, 1973, p 28). This spirit squares well with the overall philosophy of the unit/credit system ('a learner-centred, needs- and motivation-based language learning system', Trim, 1976, p 78) as well as with the notion of self-assessment.

In an article dealing with the need for objective evaluative criteria in language teaching Valdman (1971) points out that criterion-referenced tests are an integral part of programmed self-instructional materials. If the unit/credit system is going to be realized in a fashion resembling programmed instruction, which conceptually and practically is inextricably associated with individualized learning, we will of course be able to draw on the experience gained with stimulus-response drills and other rigorously structured exercises on discrete learning points. As has been pointed out, such tasks can in fact be regarded as being made up of test items each of which offers instant feedback to the learner on his performance level.

Others have expressed concern for 'the dehumanizing effect of evaluative procedures in individualized programmes' (Jorstad, 1974, referring to Giorgiades, 1973).

The general trends in adult language learning, ie greater emphasis on performance objectives, individual learning, and criterion-referenced, learner-centred evaluation, are represented in the unit/credit approach and ought to be reflected in the kinds of assessment techniques applied as well.

4.3.2 Self-assessment in relation to specific learning objectives

For a majority of adult learners in the Council of Europe member countries the evaluation of general, non-specialized language proficiency is probably more important than the evaluation of highly specialized language abilities. Most learners who seek to evaluate their performance will want to know, in the first place, what stage they have reached generally in the language, or else, what stage they have reached in relation to a certain language course they have studied. This does not mean, of course, that the evaluation of achievement within a well-defined area, or in a very specific part of a course of study, is uninteresting. On the contrary, for a good many learners such evaluation is very useful and necessary as an integral part of their learning (cf for instance, Valdman, 1971). Knowledge of one's gradual progression is always conducive to the attainment of established goals, or, as the case may be, to the realistic adjustment of one's goals. Evaluation of this kind, ie continuous assessment which helps the learner to form a clear conception of how he is progressing towards his personal objectives, should therefore be considered as a very essential feature of any major educational programme.

The kinds of methods proposed so far can be best used for global evaluation purposes. In most cases this means some sort of terminal assessment of learning. It should be pointed out, however, that the methods are not necessarily unsuitable for intermittent use, for example during a course of study which extends over a year or two. Most learners who work seriously and for some duration of time will notice gains even on these global self-assessment instruments.

4.4 Standardized forms based on T-level objectives

Forms of self-assessment, and particularly forms of continuous self-assessment, within the unit/credit system cannot be specified in great detail until it has been made possible to outline more clearly how the system is going to be implemented in actual learning programmes. That is, very detailed proposals can only be made when the nature and contents of concepts like unit and module have been given more precise definitions.

'The construction of a system for evaluation should be closely integrated with the building up of a unit/credit system and be based on the content of the units' (Conclusions, *Rüschlikon Symposium*; see Council of Europe document, 1971, p 5).

The most concrete specifications of unit/credit objectives so far are to be found in *The Threshold Level* (van Ek, 1975) and *Un Niveau-seuil* (Coste, *et al*, 1976), and therefore they will be the main points of reference in the discussions which follow. The English document, being the one most widely known to date, will be the primary source of reference.

At every stage of the development of self-management techniques it is of fundamental importance to keep the target-group learner in mind. Materials and instructions must be easy to understand and easy to handle, otherwise they may not function in the hands of those who have little academic training. This constraint prevents us from sampling freely from the T-level documents when we want to translate.

4.4.1 Topics

One sort of objectives specification that seems to lend itself quite readily to adaptation to easily comprehensible self-evaluation procedures is the behavioural specification of topics in *The Threshold Level* (van Ek, 1975, pp 22–28). This list specifies what the learner who has reached threshold level will be able to do with regard to each of the topics included in the definition of the *Threshold Level* (pp 14–16). As an example we may take Topic 1 (Personal identification) under which heading we find, among several others, the entry *name*. The behavioural specification with regard to this topic states that the learners should for instance be able to spell out their names if required. This is a very concrete performance objective which, of course, can be tested in various ways. Furthermore, most learners would have no difficulty in telling whether they could measure up to this requirement or not. The simplest way to find out would therefore seem to be to ask the straightforward question: Can you spell your name in English? or, in declarative form:

I can spell my name in English ☐ Yes   ☐ No

The average *Threshold Level* learner would check the *Yes* box, the average learner below threshold level would check the *No* box. A range of statements (a check-list) of this kind therefore ought to be a helpful guiding tool for the learner who is working towards the *Threshold Level* objectives.

Working on this assumption I devised a self-assessment form comprising 30 statements representing different topics in the *Threshold Level* specification (see Figure 5). The form was then used in a very modest try-out with a group of adult learners.

Again it should be pointed out that this kind of evaluation instrument is primarily intended for autonomous learners and others who have an interest in finding out, for themselves, their levels in relation to *Threshold Level* objectives but who do not wish to, or who cannot, take a formal, centrally administered test. It is suggested that a guideline for evaluation be supplied at the end of the form:

'If your total number of Yes crosses is twenty-five or above, and if your judgment of your own language ability is fairly accurate, you are likely to have reached threshold level in English'.

This number, twenty-five positive responses out of thirty possible, is a subjective estimate which of course would have to be empirically verified.

Note also that the test should be given in the learner's *native* language.

Instead of forcing the learner to choose between the absolute Yes/No dichotomy, it might be more rewarding to allow for some latitude of response, eg by complementing with an 'uncertain' box or by using a scale with several steps (for instance 'yes', definitely 'yes, probably', 'uncertain', 'no, probably not', 'no, definitely not'). Compare for example the attitude scales in the Appendix of Richterich and Chancerel (1977).

Figure 5: Example of self-assessment form, type D

Sample questionnaire for self-assessment at T-Level

[To be translated into the learner's native language]

Instruction: Imagine that you meet an English-speaking person from another country. He does not know anything about you and your country. Indicate your estimated command of the language by putting a cross in the appropriate box (*Yes* or *No*) for each statement.

1. I can tell him when and where I was born.	☐ Yes	☐ No
2. I can spell my name in English.	☐ Yes	☐ No
3. I can describe my home to him.	☐ Yes	☐ No
4. I can tell him what kinds of food and drink I like and don't like.	☐ Yes	☐ No
5. I can tell him about my interests (hobbies, interests in general, etc.).	☐ Yes	☐ No
6. I can tell him what I usually read (kinds of books, newspapers, magazines, textbooks, etc.).	☐ Yes	☐ No
7. I can ask him what newspapers there are in his own country.	☐ Yes	☐ No
8. I can tell him what I do in my free time.	☐ Yes	☐ No
9. I can ask him how to get to a certain place by public transport.	☐ Yes	☐ No
10. I can tell him what I think of art galleries.	☐ Yes	☐ No
11. I can ask him about the price of a ticket for a certain football match.	☐ Yes	☐ No
12. I can tell him about things that might interest a tourist in my home region.	☐ Yes	☐ No
13. I can ask him questions about traffic-rules in his own country.	☐ Yes	☐ No
14. I can say something about social security in my country (old-age pensions, medical care, etc.).	☐ Yes	☐ No
15. I can tell him what sort of government we have in my country.	☐ Yes	☐ No
16. I can say something about my political views and tell him whether I support a political party.	☐ Yes	☐ No
17. I can tell him how I feel at the moment (if I am hungry, tired, ill, etc.).	☐ Yes	☐ No
18. I can ask him to help me arrange an appointment with a doctor.	☐ Yes	☐ No
19. I can tell him that I take medicine regularly.	☐ Yes	☐ No
20. I can tell him that I am tired and need some rest.	☐ Yes	☐ No
21. I can ask him to repeat slowly what he just said.	☐ Yes	☐ No
22. I can ask him about the pronunciation of a certain word.	☐ Yes	☐ No
23. I can ask him to characterize the climate in his country.	☐ Yes	☐ No
24. I can ask him if he knows the approximate price of a certain piece of clothing in his own country.	☐ Yes	☐ No
25. I can inform him about where he can have his car serviced.	☐ Yes	☐ No
26. I can ask him to ring me up some time.	☐ Yes	☐ No
27. I can ask for his telephone number and give my own number.	☐ Yes	☐ No
28. I can tell him where he can change foreign money.	☐ Yes	☐ No
29. I can describe weather-conditions in the four seasons in my own country.	☐ Yes	☐ No
30. I can tell him where he can eat and drink.	☐ Yes	☐ No
Total number of crosses:	— Yes	— No

Evaluation: If your total number of Yes crosses is [25] or above, and if your judgement of your own language ability is fairly accurate, you are likely to have reached Threshold Level in English.

4.4.2 Functions

Another possible starting-point for discussions about self-assessment within the unit/credit framework is the specification of language functions and exponents of those functions that are found in *The Threshold Level* and *Un niveau-seuil*.

It appears that these kinds of objectives specification could be easily comprehended by the learners if combined and then adapted for self-assessment purposes in the same way as was done with the topics specification above. To illustrate, we may take the function 'inquiring about agreement or disagreement' (*ibid* p 19). The specification of language forms (exponents) lists the following items as representative of the function (*ibid* p 36):

Do you agree?
Do you think so, too?
Don't you agree?
Don't you think so?
(short questions)

In self-evaluation form this particular item might read as follows:

I can ask a person if he or she is of the same opinion as I am. (To be formulated in the learner's native language.) ☐ Yes ☐ No
Examples: Do you agree?
Don't you think so?

In *Un niveau-seuil* (Coste, *et al*, 1976) the list of functions and their most common exponents in French (*Actes de paroles/Actes d'ordres*, pp 83–224) occupies a central position. The section would seem to be well suited to the same kind of adaptation for self-assessment techniques as was proposed for the English counterpart.

4.5 Final note on self-assessment forms

To conclude this section it ought to be said that we do not ignore or underestimate the technical unreliability that affects any assessment procedure based on impressionistic estimation. Nor do we overlook the fact that unpredictable personality variables such as varying degrees of self-confidence, perceptiveness, and general ability to form valid judgements may be important factors. Naturally none of these traits co-varies with linguistic ability and therefore we must acknowledge that in certain extreme cases the learner will get nothing out of using purely subjective assessment methods. On the other hand it is probably fair to say that it is only a small minority of learners whose abilities to perceive and discern deviates so markedly from 'the norm' that their judgement of foreign language standards is of no value at all. Secondly, evaluation by means of subjective questionnaires is only seen as one variety of self-assessment procedure. Others include assessment in autonomous groups or between peers, self-observation in authentic language situations, self-tests through exposure to mass-media (radio and television broadcasts, newspapers, tapes, cassettes, records, etc), the use of self-administered conventional tests with keys (see Section 4.6). Impressionistic self-assessment by means of questionnaires etc ought to be seen as a complement to such methods.

Our idea, therefore, is not to substitute self-assessment procedures for objective formal tests, but rather to aim at an optimal combination of the two approaches. Both have their merits – self-assessment for being learner-centred and potentially capable of taking the aural/oral aspects into full account, and formal tests for being more reliable (at least in the technical sense of the word) and better known. It therefore seems that our aim should be to try to strike a happy balance between the two.

4.6 Self-assessment by means of formal tests

4.6.1 Assessment of general language proficiency

The most common self-assessment aid, apart from the opportunities for tacit self-observation that pattern drill types of exercises and programmed self-instructional materials offer, consists of conventional written tasks accompanied by a list of correct answers which the learner goes through after having completed all the items. Especially at the beginning stages of learning such tasks need to be of the multiple-choice type, so that no uncertainty as to the correctness of any particular answer arises. Open-ended questions and free production tasks are more difficult to supply with simple answer models. Often it is quite impossible to anticipate all possible and correct responses; usually some responses are more correct, or more wrong, than others (which motivates a system of varying values). However, fill-in-the-blank and other variants of short completion tasks can be used to the extent that the test constructor can predetermine alternative, acceptable responses.

4.6.2 Assessment of specific language behaviours

Discrete-item multiple-choice tests can confidently be said to measure general language proficiency quite well, provided they are prepared and evaluated in a professional manner. When it comes to the diagnostic measurement of detailed behavioural objectives they are not quite as adequate, however. As has been explained by Clark (1972), part of the reason for this lies in 'the difficulty of identifying within a given item a specific linguistic feature whose knowledge by the student is both necessary and sufficient for a correct response' (p 239). Another reason is the fact that in a multiple-choice of *general language proficiency* you are interested in the total score, regardless of what combination of items it has been obtained by, whereas in a test of discrete language behaviour you want to know whether the candidate actually masters each of the specific competencies which the individual items purport to measure. If the test is of the multiple-choice format, the chance factor may preclude any conclusions about component abilities even if the total score is relatively high. Valid tests of performance objectives should therefore represent, as faithfully as possible, the very language behaviour that the test intends to measure, ie in most cases they should require the candidate to speak and write his responses.

4.6.3 Self-administration of Threshold Level tests

Self-administration of parallel forms of the threshold level test would seem to be an obvious area for the development of self-assessment practices within the framework of the unit/credit system. To the extent that so-called objective, or rather objectively scoreable, test types are used, one would only need to provide the learner with simple answer sheets of the sorts discussed earlier.

Learner administration and self-scoring of productive (subjective) tests, for instance an oral test involving recording of responses on magnetic tape, is of course a much more problem-laden undertaking. If the learner were to be provided with a spoken model (a printed model would of course be inappropriate), he would have to compare and make distinctions between aural stimuli, which is not an easy matter for anyone at threshold level. Assistance by a fellow learner, or a group of fellow learners, might make such evaluation easier.

Likewise, application of the principle of learner-centred evaluation to tests of free productive writing creates some thorny problems. It has been proposed that writing a letter requesting information about accommodation in England be included in the English threshold level test. Even such a well-defined task could no doubt be solved in innumerable ways, which means that a handy standard model would be very difficult to produce. The feasibility of the undertaking depends of course to a great extent upon what degree of formal perfection should be expected of the learner. If the criterion is 'having got the message across', no matter in what form, then the evaluation part might not be too difficult to master for a fellow learner, for instance. If, on the other hand, a certain degree of stylistic sophistication is considered important, then a fellow learner is not in a very good position to judge.

A test of oral communication ability (with emphasis on communication), eg through a structured interview (which has been suggested) or some such procedure, could theoretically be handled by a fellow learner, or by a group of fellow learners, possibly in some manner similar to those described in Section 2.5. Very great care would of course have to be taken to ensure that the necessary instructions were specific enough. It would also be helpful to compare, under controlled conditions, results obtained by learner-evaluation and results obtained by regular outside administration of the same test. The outcome could help us determine the usefulness of this kind of peer-evaluation. It is therefore proposed that the follow-up activities of this project include some research on this point.

4.6.4 Formal tests based on the Threshold Level specifications of words and structures

In Section 4.4 above we tried to outline some unconventional approaches to evaluation based on the topics, functions and exponent categories set out in *The Threshold Level*. Both the English and the French threshold level documents (van Ek, 1975, and Coste, *et al*, 1976, respectively) also contain specifications of the words and grammatical structures that are most likely to be employed in T-level courses. Although the advisability of such a measure may be rightly questioned, it is of course quite possible to devise formal self-assessment tests on these words and structures. With proper instructions, and *in combination with other techniques*, such tests might serve a useful purpose.

4.7 Informal self-assessment

The self-assessment methods that we have dealt with so far are more or less formal in nature, ie they all imply some carefully predetermined course of action or some requisite printed aid. In addition to this approach to assessment, many informal assessment methods suggest themselves. Some of these are probably more expedient and effective than the most sophisticated formal testing technique, others are only of very limited significance. Since it would be beyond the scope of the present study to try to establish a comprehensive typology of such informal assessment strategies, we will limit ourselves to commenting briefly on a few that seem to have obvious practical relevance for our purposes.

4.7.1 Informal self-assessment in a group

The learner's assessment of his own language ability can be greatly facilitated if he is a member of a group with which he can interact. The group can assist in various ways, eg by informally discussing each member's proficiency level or progress rate (this requires a certain atmosphere of mutual trust in the group), or by providing a framework for role-play and similar communicative exercises. The group does not need to be big; even two people can be called a group for the purposes we are discussing here.

Evaluative group activities of the kinds which are our present concern should take as their starting-point the objectives stated in relevant Council of Europe documents (eg van Ek, 1975; Coste, et al, 1976). Since these objectives are generally quite explicit, it should be possible to carry out a great deal of communicative 'test exercises' in accordance with unit/credit aims. In principle this would mean that the performance objectives were acted out as communication tasks. Necessary prompts could be supplied in various ways, eg by means of the native language or pictures. The participants in the communication acts would have to decide, either subjectively or by some other principle, whether the intended verbal functions had been achieved.

Autonomous interaction practice in simulated situations can range in degree of complexity from very short exchanges of greetings ('socializing'; van Ek, 1975, p 44) to a group discussion on a topic of current interest ('expressing and finding out intellectual and emotional attitudes'; *ibid* pp 36–42). As for evaluation, most learners would no doubt be able to tell whether their own standards permitted them to interact adequately in each situation. If not, a group discussion or consultation with a fellow learner, would be helpful in most cases. Such discussions could even be turned into a semi-formal evaluation procedure if each member of the group assesses all the others, resulting in a consensus opinion for each (rather like a skating competition). For obvious reasons, this method cannot be applied without due preparation in the group. Most adults are very sensitive to openly pronounced value judgements about themselves, and therefore it is imperative that any testing activity, be it formal or informal, is expressly approved of by each individual member of the group.

Role-playing and other communication tasks should be practised continuously almost from the beginning in any orally oriented language course. As we mentioned earlier, the exact techniques to be used depend to some extent on what types of learning programmes the unit/credit system is going to embody.

4.7.2 Informal self-assessment in authentic situations

Authentic language situations provide the most valid opportunities for self-evaluation. It is in the actual use of the language, in real-life settings, that one may ultimately test one's communicative ability. Therefore the learner should always try to assess his ability in terms of his use of the language in natural situations, not in terms of test scores or in terms of performance in an artificial learning situation. Proper questions to ask oneself are: How well do I understand this letter, this newspaper headline, this information leaflet, this telephone message, this television interview? How well can I make myself understood when talking to somebody in the foreign language? Can I express my intentions, my feelings, my thoughts? It is less useful to ask: How many of the words in my textbook do I know? How well do I master this structural pattern? How foreign is my accent? etc.

It is hoped that further work in the field will include attempts at developing methods for self-assessment in authentic language situations.

COUNCIL
OF EUROPE

CONSEIL
DE L' EUROPE

7 CHAPTER SEVEN: 7

TEACHER TRAINING

INTRODUCTION TO CHAPTER SEVEN

The novelty of the proposals developed by the Council of Europe Project Group has not only led to the production of new learning materials but also to widespread reflection on the nature, aims and methods of teacher training. The experimental implementation of these proposals has, in several cases, included the introduction of new teacher-training schemes. These schemes have, on the whole, been developed on the spot, to meet the requirements of various pilot projects. The role of the members of the Project Group has been that of observers rather than initiators. As in the field of methodology, a rich fund of experience has now been accumulated, on the basis of which an international Project Group can play a more directly stimulating and guiding role. In the follow-up project, to be initiated late in 1982, teacher training will be a major focus of orientation. The following extract deals with a number of key issues that will engage the attention of the new Project Group.

Extract VII

from C Edelhoff in: *Modern Languages (1971–1981)*

Purposes and Needs for teacher training

The Modern Languages Project systems development proposals are not limited to certain aspects of language teaching alone. They encompass indeed the whole area of pedagogy and classroom management in the teaching of foreign and second languages. This is why the purposes of teacher training must be described as acts of adult professional learning in

(i)   attitudes,
(ii) knowledge, and
(iii) skills,

and not only in methodology.

(i) Attitudes

Teachers teaching a communication curriculum must be ready to accept that communication is free interaction between people of all talents, views, races and socio-cultural backgrounds and that foreign-language communication, especially, is there for international understanding, human rights, democratic development and individual enrichment. This requires, therefore, above all an attitude of open-mindedness, self-determination and respect for others, their history, environment, attitudes and views. Furthermore, the very nature of free communication demands an attitude of respect towards the learner and his or her needs as well as a readiness to regard one aim of teaching being to enable learners to develop their talents in a self-directed way both as members of groups and as individuals.

Thirdly, the teacher is required to regard language learning as everybody's right instead of the privilege of an elite. He is, moreover, expected to look at language not only as form but, first and foremost, as a means of communication and a system of meaning rather than as external form. This places meaning and acceptability before formal correctness.

The teacher, therefore, will be aware that his own role in foreign-language communication is not different from that of the learners in principle but only in degree.

This finally, will only be possible if the teacher is prepared to look at learning, including his own learning, as a never-ending process of continuing endeavour and enrichment.

(ii) Knowledge

It is obvious that all this requires the teachers to have specific knowledge of the nature of learning, of the learners and their conditioning, of both the mother tongue and the target language and the socio-cultural connotations.

(iii) Skills

The skills of the teacher will have to match attitudes and knowledge so that he or she is able to understand 'learner-centredness, the idea of needs, the role of assessment, self-directed learning, the relations between language as tool of communication and language as system, the concept of learning strategy, the concept of functional teaching, the idea that all mistakes are logical'. (Porcher, L. 1980b).

Competence in the target language seems to be of greatest importance in this respect. This includes communication skills which enable the teacher to 'share meanings, experiences and affects' (Breen/Candlin) rather than be limited to the knowledge and handling of the formal system alone.

Skills must also be developed for managing classroom interaction as communication and the teacher must be able to apply and develop new methods to this end. He is expected to handle new materials and media and to use and develop new methods of evaluation.

It is important to note, however, that materials and methodology have never been known to be a closed and perfect system of the management of teaching but have always been part of the experimentation itself. The overall skill, then, to be achieved by way of trial and error and constant participation in experimentation is that of handling innovation, not a set of recipe rules.

Pre-service teacher training

It would be short-sighted if one were to leave training for change only to in-service measures. Indeed, the most effective changes have always come from younger teachers in schools who have been trained in a new or modified way. This is why pre-service teacher training, too, must be considered in the light of the Council of Europe Modern Languages Project.

The training of foreign-language teachers at European universities or university-like institutions is based on a combination of complex considerations, academic, professional and political, which seem to differ greatly from country to country. Yet there is a great deal of common ground. Basically most academic courses for language teachers tend to be detached from school life. It is a commonly shared experience of the European language-teaching force that the young teacher leaving college has to cope with what has come to be called the "shock of practice". Moreover, in many countries a significant section of the language teaching body is trained in the academic tradition of higher education leading to better reputed and more highly paid positions than those open to the majority, who take shorter and less academic courses. It is difficult to judge which of the two streams that can be discerned in many countries enables teachers to become the better communication oriented language teachers.

Professional considerations of welding theory and practice require a life-long study and learning process on the part of the language teacher. If their detachment from practical matters is going to be overcome, pre-service training agencies will have to define their role in this continuum with regard to syllabus and materials design, textbook and test analysis, classroom interaction and tactics as well as evaluation. At the same time those charged with in-service procedures must be aware of a need to evaluate and investigate the theoretical implications of practical teaching matters.

Obviously the implications of change in many countries are manifold and beyond the reach of the Council of Europe Project. The most general aspect of this seems to be bridging the gap between administrative structures of the universities and the educational systems respectively, at least in the area of teacher training, syllabus design and materials development and evaluation.

In-service teacher education and training

The principle of lifelong learning, well established by the Council of Europe adult education projects in recent years, implies that all in-service training activities must build upon the teachers' *present* attitudes, knowledge, objectives and methods.

Firstly, this requires us to elicit an awareness of and confrontation with the teachers' own fears, preconceptions and teacher role definitions, their perceived situational constraints, their own social and communicative behaviour in groups, an awareness and consideration of alternatives and choice. This is why teachers have to be involved in the search for and proposal of solutions to their perceived problems and constraints in their teaching situation. Teachers will hardly be prepared or able to administer autonomous learning processes in their students if their own learning is not geared to the same principle.

It follows, secondly, that clear justifications for communicative language teaching (as opposed to other approaches) must be given by way of presenting the main objective of language teaching and learning as being the sharing of meanings, experiences and affects. The teacher should be enabled to regard communication as the means of sharing and as a relationship between grammar, phonology, vocabulary, functions and notions as well as social behaviour. These elements should not be regarded as discrete, nor should one of them be considered to be of "more importance" than any other.

Finally, in-service training must enable the teacher to encourage the learner to become actively involved, to stop being frightened of making mistakes, to take initiative, to progress towards self-management and independence and to develop social involvement and co-operation in the classroom.

Very often this will necessarily lead to the reassessment of traditional views of the role of grammar, pronunciation and spelling rules, the exclusive use of literary texts and classical testing techniques. Using the target language on in-service training courses has proved to be an important vehicle for bringing this about. Role-play and simulation as well as other language activities have shown to be very effective, too.

The biggest impact, however, can only be achieved by in-service training measures that engage teachers in learning and developing activities permanently or at least over a longer period of time.

Owing to the fact that the conditions and constraints will differ, in some respects greatly, between or indeed within member countries experimentation will have to cover different forms of organization, ie

— Individual teacher (in-service) training (reading and studying, multi-media courses on radio and television);
— Individual and group teacher (in-service) training (at local, regional and central levels; in ad hoc seminars and courses; in regular and permanent working groups, afternoon and residential meetings);
— Pooling together different agencies and institutions at local and central levels, including bi-national and international, pre-service and in-service organizations;
— Establishing an international pool of experiences and models and teaching/learning materials and information sources.

COUNCIL
OF EUROPE

CONSEIL
DE L' EUROPE

CONCLUSION

CONCLUSION

The work summarized in this reader has had a considerable impact, not only in Europe but on a global scale. The European unit-credit scheme for language learning by adults has not materialized, at any rate at the time of writing, and there seems no prospect of its introduction in the immediate future. Technically, a number of schemes are feasible, as set out in Trim (1977), from a 'weak' scheme in which different teaching and examining authorities would situate their syllabus in a common framework and agree credit ratings for an educational passport, to a 'strong' scheme in which some existing or specially created agency would itself issue internationally recognized certificates and diplomas. There are few, if any, signs that the many existing agencies in the field would agree to hand over responsibilities to such a body, or that the member governments of the Council of Europe would countenance its establishment. Official opinion may of course change, but in response to changes in the political climate rather than purely educational considerations.

It should however be clear to the reader that the central concerns of the Council of Europe's modern languages projects are not necessarily bound to a formal unit-credit scheme. The basic aim has been, and remains, to develop a framework of concepts within which learners, teachers and the other 'partners for learning' can plan their work more effectively and co-operate more closely, concretely and insightfully. If the language teaching profession is to rise to the challenge of the times, it has to shuffle off the attitudes, values and practices of the past, when a knowledge of language was a badge of a cultural elite, and devote itself wholeheartedly to the task of making the broad masses of our population willing and able to communicate with their neighbours. A long and steadfast campaign of educational innovation and renewal is needed and we are still in its relatively early stages. Structures have to be changed or newly created. Syllabuses have to be set up. Examinations have to be reformed, new materials produced and new classroom teaching methods developed. All these developments are under way, with considerable variations in pace and extent from one country to another and from one educational sector to another, according to the nature of the educational systems, available resources, national and local traditions and practices, etc. The sense of common purpose and interest is growing as the consensus of informed opinion becomes stronger.

As the project has matured, the concepts and models described in this reader have been put to work in pilot projects in many countries and in different educational fields. An overall survey is made in the Final Report of CDCC Project no. 4, entitled 'Modern Languages 1971–1981'. A school interaction network was established, co-ordinated by R Bergentoft (Sweden), bringing together teachers engaged in the experimental teaching of languages for communication in most CDCC countries. A similar but smaller network of centres engaged in language teaching for migrant workers and their families was reported in a compendium of studies edited by T Jupp (UK). Further compendia have been produced on: 14 methodological experiments in communicative teaching, edited with an important introduction by D Coste as *Towards a renewal of language learning and teaching: some current work in Europe; Analyses of language needs*, edited by R Richterich; *Teacher-training programmes according with the principles of the Council of Europe Modern Language Project*, edited by H-J Krumm. The findings of Project 4 were considered by an inter-governmental conference in

Strasbourg in February 1982 and by the CDCC in June of that year. The resulting resolutions formed the basis of Recommendation (81) 18 of the Committee of Ministers of the Council of Europe. The Recommendation will undoubtedly set the direction of educational policy on modern language teaching in the coming years. The text is reproduced as Appendix A.

The CDCC included in its programme a new project – Project 12: 'Learning and teaching languages for communication'. It will in many ways continue the work of Project 4 in accordance with the ideas set out in this reader. The most important practical task will be to bring the attitudes, concept and methods into the classroom. A few high-level decisions by central authorities are not enough. Teachers and learners should fully understand and accept the aims, objectives and methods of the learning/teaching programme they are involved in, rather than blindly follow a course imposed on them. Even better, they should be involved directly in negotiating its content and methodology. But how is that state of affairs to be brought about? If the mass of learners and teachers are to be willing and able to replace existing aims and methods by new ones, then:

– learners must find the new methods successful and enjoyable, and understand and accept the basis of aims and methods;
– teachers must be convinced that the new ways of working will be more effective and provide greater job satisfaction;
– new tasks must not be simply an extra load, but must supersede less appropriate ones;
– the new way of working must be compatible with the constraints necessarily imposed by the nature of the education system within which they have to operate;
– the new objectives and methods should be required or at least encouraged by central curricular guidelines, syllabuses and qualifying examinations;
– appropriate teaching materials must be available on an adequate scale;
– teachers must be properly prepared for the new tasks facing them; this implies radical changes in the pattern of initial teacher preparation as well as an intensified programme of in-service training.

There may be as many as a quarter of a million language teachers in Europe, most of them trained (if at all) in a very different tradition. It is out of the question for an international body to attempt to train numbers of that order. A programme of up to 30 workshops for teacher trainers is therefore planned for 1984–86. The 1,000 or so teacher trainers involved may then reach a high proportion of practising teachers.

Ideas do not, however, stand still. The reader should not gain the impression that the ideas presented here are in a final, immutable form or that intellectual development has ceased, leaving only a practical job of dissemination and implementation to be done. It is certain that ideas and models will be stretched and modified – perhaps profoundly – when the attempt is made to apply them to the diverse conditions of the real world. Each time that the Threshold Level model is applied to a new language, it is adapted and enriched. We shall continue our attempt to develop a more comprehensive model for specifying communicative objectives, especially at higher educational levels. What should, say, a mature school-leaver's or a university graduate's language proficiency be? We need to examine carefully how to provide language learners with 'cultural competence', the largely tacit assumptions and knowledge, shared attitudes, values and beliefs current in the community, which a member of a particular society brings to the act of communication and in the light of which he directs and interprets his experience. The 'culture gap' may be at least as important in disrupting communication as formal linguistic errors of various kinds. A profession concerned with facilitating international communication cannot ignore this dimension.

As objectives become more clearly formulated, attention is also turning from the products of communication and of learning to the processes. We need to know what we are aiming at, but then to remember that at every point in a learning programme we are forming – or deforming – the learner's ability and willingness to communicate. Ends and means are inextricably interwoven. Moreover, as we have seen, it is the strategies of communication the learner has to acquire as well as its content.

In short, the Council of Europe's modern language projects have still a great deal of hard work before them.

J L Trim

COUNCIL OF EUROPE
COMMITTEE OF MINISTERS

RECOMMENDATION No. R (82) 18

**OF THE COMMITTEE OF MINISTERS TO MEMBER STATES
CONCERNING MODERN LANGUAGES**

*(Adopted by the Committee of Ministers on 24 September 1982
at the 350th meeting of the Ministers' Deputies)*

The Committee of Ministers, under the terms of Article 15.*b* of the Statute of the Council of Europe,

Considering that the aim of the Council of Europe is to achieve greater unity between its members and that this aim can be pursued in particular by the adoption of common action in the cultural field ;

Bearing in mind the European Cultural Convention signed in Paris on 19 December 1954 ;

Having regard to its Resolution (69) 2 of 25 January 1969 on an intensified modern language teaching programme for Europe ;

Recalling Recommendation 814 (1977) of the Assembly concerning modern languages in Europe ;

Having noted the report "Modern languages : 1971-81" drawn up by Project Group No. 4 of the Council for Cultural Co-operation ;

Having noted the work of the Conference entitled "Across the threshold towards multi-lingual Europe—Vivre le multilinguisme européen", which was organised by the Council of Europe in Strasbourg from 23 to 26 February 1982 ;

Considering that the rich heritage of diverse languages and cultures in Europe is a valuable common resource to be protected and developed, and that a major educational effort is needed to convert that diversity from a barrier to communication into a source of mutual enrichment and understanding ;

Considering that it is only through a better knowledge of European modern languages that it will be possible to facilitate communication and interaction among Europeans of different mother tongues in order to promote European mobility, mutual understanding and co-operation, and overcome prejudice and discrimination ;

Considering that member states, when adopting or developing national policies in the field of modern language learning and teaching, may achieve greater convergence at the European level, by means of appropriate arrangements for ongoing co-operation and co-ordination of policies,

Recommends the governments of member states, in the framework of their national educational policies and systems, and national cultural development policies, to implement by all available means and within the limits of available resources, the measures set out in the appendix to the present recommendation ;

195

Requests the governments of member states to convey this recommendation and the reference document which forms its basis,[1] through appropriate national channels, to the attention of competent public and private bodies in their countries.

Appendix to Recommendation No. R (82) 18

**Measures to be implemented concerning
the learning and teaching of modern languages**

A. *General measures*

1.   To ensure, as far as possible, that all sections of their populations have access to effective means of acquiring a knowledge of the languages of other member states (or of other communities within their own country) as well as the skills in the use of those languages that will enable them to satisfy their communicative needs and in particular :

1.1. to deal with the business of everyday life in another country, and to help foreigners staying in their own country to do so ;

1.2. to exchange information and ideas with young people and adults who speak a different language and to communicate their thoughts and feelings to them ;

1.3. to achieve a wider and deeper understanding of the way of life and forms of thought of other peoples and of their cultural heritage.

2.   To promote, encourage and support the efforts of teachers and learners at all levels to apply in their own situation the principles of the construction of language-learning systems (as these are progressively developed within the Council of Europe "Modern languages" programme) :

2.1. by basing language teaching and learning on the needs, motivations, characteristics and resources of learners ;

2.2. by defining worthwhile and realistic objectives as explicitly as possible ;

2.3. by developing appropriate methods and materials ;

2.4. by developing suitable forms and instruments for the evaluation of learning programmes.

3.   To promote research and development programmes leading to the introduction, at all educational levels, of methods and materials best suited to enabling different classes and types of student to acquire a communicative proficiency appropriate to their specific needs.

B. *Language learning in schools*

4.   To encourage the teaching of at least one European language other than the national language or the vehicular language of the area concerned to pupils from the age of ten or the point at which they enter secondary education (or earlier according to national or local situations) with adequate time allocation and in such a way as to enable them by the end of the period of compulsory schooling, within the limits set by their individual ability, to use the language effectively for communication with other speakers of that language, both in transacting the business of everyday living and in building social and personal relations, on the basis of mutual understanding of, and respect for, the cultural identity of others.

5.   To make provision for the diversification of language study in schools :

5.1. by making it possible for pupils, wherever appropriate, to study more than one European or other modern language ;

5.2. by ensuring the availability, according to local circumstances, of facilities for learning as wide a range of languages as possible.

---

1. Report "Modern languages : 1971-81".

6.   To promote international contacts by individual pupils and classes through exchanges, study visits abroad and other means.

C. *Language learning in upper secondary school, higher education, further education and adult education*

7.   To encourage educational institutions to provide facilities for the continuation of language learning by all students in upper secondary, higher and further education, as appropriate to their special fields of work and study, in order to facilitate international professional mobility and co-operation at all levels.

8.   To ensure that adequate resources are available to enable students who have completed their full-time education to acquire further knowledge of languages in accordance with their professional, social and personal needs and motivations.

9.   To take all the measures necessary to enable adults who have had hitherto little or no chance of learning a modern language to acquire the ability to use a modern language for communicative purposes.

D. *Language learning by migrants and their families*

10.   To promote the provision of adequate facilities for migrant workers and the members of their families :

10.1. to acquire sufficient knowledge of the language of the host community for them to play an active part in the working, political and social life of that community, and in particular to enable the children of migrants to acquire a proper education and to prepare them for the transition from full-time education to work ;

10.2. to develop their mother tongues both as educational and cultural instruments and in order to maintain and improve their links with their culture of origin.

11.   To promote the introduction and development of appropriate initial and further training programmes for teachers of languages to migrants, leading to recognised qualifications.

12.   To participate in the development of language programmes involving co-operation between authorities or other bodies representing the host community, the migrant community and the country of origin, especially with regard to the production of teaching materials, teacher training and mother tongue development.

E. *Initial and further teacher training*

13.   To promote the development and introduction of methods for such initial and further training of teachers of modern languages as will enable them to develop the attitudes and acquire the knowledge, skills and techniques necessary to teach languages effectively for communicative purposes, for example by :

13.1. considering the extent to which the pattern of modern language studies in higher education provides an adequate preparation for future language teachers ;

13.2. providing facilities through bilateral and multilateral agreements for all future teachers to spend a substantial period of their course of study in a country where the language they will teach is spoken as a mother tongue ;

13.3. contributing to an intensified programme of in-service teacher training, including internationally organised, staffed and recruited in-service courses for language teachers, and facilitating the participation of serving teachers in such courses ;

13.4. promoting stays at regular intervals by serving teachers in the countries whose languages they teach.

F. *International co-operation*

14.   To promote the national and international collaboration of governmental and non-governmental institutions engaged in the development of methods of teaching and evaluation in the field of modern language learning and in the production and use of materials, including institutions engaged in the production and use of multi-media material.

15.   To encourage by all appropriate means, taking into account their particular status, radio and television bodies to co-operate with those in other member states in the planning, production and exploitation of modern language learning programmes as well as of documentaries on life, society and culture in the countries where the language being learnt is spoken.

16.   To consider means of international co-operation for monitoring the quality of language teaching materials and courses.

17.   To take such steps as are necessary to complete the establishment of an effective European system of information exchange covering all aspects of language learning, teaching and research, and making full use of advanced information technology.

18.   To ensure, as far as possible, that programmes which implement measures set out in the different chapters of this recommendation are notified to the Council for Cultural Co-operation, and that government-sponsored programmes contain provision wherever possible for consultation and co-operation between the agencies concerned and their counterparts in other member states.

APPENDIX B: BIBLIOGRAPHY[1]

Council of Europe publications and documents
issued in connection with Project No. 4

Alexander, L G (1977): *Some methodological implications of Waystage and Threshold Level*, Council of Europe, CCC/EES (77) 13.

Bergentoft, R (1983): *Consolidated report on the interaction network of the school sector of the Modern Languages Project, September 1979–May 1981*, Council of Europe, CDCC (81) 35.

Bung, K (1973a): *The foreign language needs of waiters and hotel staff*, Council of Europe, CCC/EES (73) 16 rev.

Bung, K (1973b): *The specification of objectives in a language-learning system for adults*, Council of Europe, CCC/EES (73) 34.

Chaplen, E F (1975): *Measuring achievement in adult language learning*, Council of Europe, CCC/EES (75) 73.

Coste, D, Courtillon, J, Ferenczi, V, Martins-Baltar, M, Papo, E, (CREDIF) and Roulet, E (1976): *Un niveau-seuil*, Council of Europe. Published 1981 by Hatier, Paris.

Coste, D, (ed) (1982): *Contributions to a renewal of language learning and teaching – some current work in Europe*, Council of Europe.

van Ek J A (1973): 'The 'threshold level' in a unit/credit system' in *Systems development in adult language learning*, Council of Europe. Published 1980 under the same title, Pergamon, Oxford.

van Ek, J A (1975): *The Threshold Level*, Council of Europe. Published 1980 as *Threshold Level English*, Pergamon, Oxford.

van Ek, J A (1976): *The threshold level for modern language learning in schools*, Council of Europe. Published 1977 by Longman, London.

van Ek, J A and Alexander, L G (1977): *Waystage*, Council of Europe. Published 1980 as *Waystage English*, Pergamon, Oxford.

van Ek, J A (1979): *Report* on the Hässelby Colloquy on 'The teaching of the language of the host country to adult migrants', Council of Europe, DECS/EES (79) 41.

A European unit/credit system for modern language learning by adults (1978) Articles taken from the review 'Education and Culture', No. 28, Council of Europe.

A European unit/credit system for modern language learning by adults, report of the Ludwigshafen Symposium, (1979), Council of Europe.

Galli de' Paratesi, N (1981): *Livello soglia per l'insegnamento dell' italiano come lingua straniera*, Council of Europe.

Gardner, P H and Winslow, J D (to be published): *Report on the SCHML research project on present and proposed methods of determining the needs of students joining courses in public sector higher education containing a significant language element*, Council of Europe.

Groot, P and Harrison, A (to be published): *A specimen test of threshold level proficiency in English*, Council of Europe.

Harrison, A (1979): *Techniques for evaluating a learner's ability to apply threshold level proficiency to every day communication*, Council of Europe, DECS/EES (79) 77.

Holec, H (1980): *Autonomy and foreign language learning*, Council of Europe. Published 1981 under the same title, Pergamon, Oxford.

Hughes, M N (1977): *Foreign language learning: European civil servants*, Council of Europe, CCC/EES (77) 27.

James, C V and Rouve, S (1973) *Survey of Curricula and Performance in Modern Languages 1971–72*, Centre for Educational Technology, University of Sussex, and Centre for Information on Language Teaching and Research, London.

Jessen, J (to be published): *Et taerskelniveau for dansk*, Council of Europe.

Jupp, T (to be published) *Consolidated report on pilot projects concerning the teaching of the language of the host country to migrants* (provisional title) (Council of Europe).

Krumm, H-J (1983) *Compendium of teacher training programmes corresponding to the principles of the Modern Languages Project* (provisional title) (Council of Europe).

Kuhn, M (1975): *On the preparation of educational material*, Council of Europe, CCC/EES (75) 1.

Martins-Baltar, M, Bourgain, D, Coste, D, Ferenczi, V and Mochet, M-A (1979): *L'écrit et les écrits: problèmes d'analyse et considérations didactiques*, Council of Europe. Published 1981 by Hatier, Paris.

Modern language learning in adult education, Report of the Rüschlikon Symposium, Council of Europe, CCC/EES (71) 135.

Oskarsson, M (1978): *Approaches to self-assessment in foreign language learning*, Council of Europe. Published 1980 under the same title, Pergamon, Oxford.

Porcher, L (1980a): *Petit guide d'emploi pour l'adaptation de 'Un niveau-seuil' pour des contextes scolaires*, Council of Europe.

[1]This bibliography first appeared in *Modern Languages (1971–1981)*, Report of CDCC Project Group 4, Council of Europe, 1981.

Porcher, L (1980b): *Reflections on language needs in the school*, Council of Europe.

Porcher, L, Huart, M and Mariet, F (CREDIF) (1980): *Adaptation de 'Un niveau-seuil' pour des contextes scolaires*, Council of Europe. Published 1982 by Havier, Paris.

Porcher, L, Barbe, G, Naymark, J, (CREDIF) and Richterich, R (to be published): *Identification des besoins langagiers de travailleurs migrants en France*, Council of Europe.

Porcher, L and Cortes, J, with Barbe, G, Bassour, A, Courtillon, J, Maillet, B, Martins-Baltar, M, Mochet, M-A, Monzauge, J and Papo, E, (CREDIF) (to be published): *Propositions pour la définition d'objectifs intermédiaires d'apprentissage du français à destination des travailleurs migrants*, Council of Europe.

Richterich, R (1973a): 'Analytical classification of the categories of adults needing to learn foreign languages' in *Systems development in adult language learning*, Council of Europe. Published 1980 under the same title, Pergamon, Oxford.

Richterich, R (1973b): 'A model for the definition of language needs of adults' in *Systems development in adult language learning*. Published 1980 under the same title, Pergamon, Oxford.

Richterich, R and Chancerel, J-L (1978): *Identifying the needs of adults learning a foreign language*, Council of Europe. Published 1980 under the same title, Pergamon, Oxford.

Richterich, R (ed) (1983): *Case studies in identifying language needs*, Pergamon, Oxford.

Roulet, E (1977): *Un niveau-seuil – présentation et guide d'emploi*, Council of Europe.

Schneider, G, Baldegger, M, Müller, M and Näf, A (1980): *Kontaktschwelle: Deutsch als Fremdsprache*, Council of Europe. Published 1981 by Langescheidt, Munich.

Slagter, P J (1979): *Un nivel umbral*, Council of Europe.

Studies on a comprehensive framework for the definition of language learning objectives (to be published, provisional title) Council of Europe.

Trim, J L M (1973a): *Consolidated report on modern languages in adult education*, Council of Europe, EES/Symp 57,3.

Trim, J L M (1973b): 'Draft outline of a European unit/credit system for modern language learning by adults' in *Systems development in adult language learning*, Council of Europe. Published 1980 under the same title, Pergamon, Oxford.

Trim, J L M (1973c): *Report* on the St. Wolfgang Symposium, 'Modern languages in adult education', EES/Symp 57.10 Council of Europe.

Trim, J L M (1974a): *Provisional suggestions regarding multimedia systems for language teaching to adults*, Council of Europe, CCC/EES (74) 3.

Trim, J L M (1974b): *Report* on the meetings of an *ad hoc* working group on the establishment of a master inventory of categories for use in the specification of objectives in a European unit/credit system for modern language learning by adults, Council of Europe, CCC/EES (74) 37.

Trim, J L M (1976): *Report* on the London Colloquy of producers and organisers of multimedia language courses on 'A European unit/credit system for modern language learning by adults', Council of Europe, CCC/EES (76) 31.

Trim, J L M (1978): *Some possible lines of development of an overall structure for a European unit/credit scheme for foreign language learning by adults*, Council of Europe. Published 1980 as *Developing a unit-credit scheme of adult language learning*, Pergamon, Oxford.

Wilkins, D A (1973): 'The linguistic and situational content of the common core in a unit/credit system' in *Systems development in adult language learning*, Council of Europe. Published 1980 under the same title, Pergamon, Oxford.